NONVERBAL BEHAVIOR IN THE CAREER INTERVIEW

Pragmatics & Beyond

An Interdisciplinary Series of Language Studies

IV:4

Walburga von Raffler-Engel

The Perception of Nonverbal behavior in the career interview

THE PERCEPTION OF NONVERBAL BEHAVIOR IN THE CAREER INTERVIEW

Walburga von Raffler-Engel
Vanderbilt University

JOHN BENJAMINS PUBLISHING COMPANY
AMSTERDAM/PHILADELPHIA

1983

304743

TABLE OF CONTENTS

PREFACE

This book explores how the nonverbal behavior of a job applicant is interpreted by the person who interviews him. It probably raises more questions than it answers and it is my sincere hope that it will stimulate further research in perception.

The book presents the findings from a series of research projects conducted over a period of three years. It grew quite pragmatically as one project led into the next. Sometimes I wanted to verify the results by approaching the subject from a different angle. This proved very fruitful as the results obtained in this manner reinforced each other. At other times, I wanted to look into some more aspects of the matter which emerged from the very research that had just been completed. This offered new insights which clarified the whole subject. I could have easily gone on for another three years. And this not only because the subject matter continued to fascinate me. The work was also great fun because of the many intelligent, imaginative, and enthusiastic students that worked with me and without whose help the research projects would never have been completed. To these young people I would like to dedicate the book:

Elizabeth B. Battey	Gina C. McNeal
Lisa M. Collins	Keith W. Newman
Frank E. Gantz III	Judy D. Olin
William P. Glasgow	Jeffrey J. Rothschild
Tyler H. Harrison	Leonard Silverstein
Charles L. Huddleston	Eiko Taguchi
Steven G. McKnight	Chandra C. Taylor

The research would have also been impossible to accomplish without the technical assistance of the following staff members at the Vanderbilt University Learning Resources Center: Dr. Penelope A. Pierce, director; George R. Foster, Jr., head technician; and Diane M. Snyder, media specialist. Penny, Robin, and Diane gave freely of their time and considerable expertise.

I also wish to thank Ms. Fay Renardson who during all the years that this research was ongoing did all the typing, using her fine sense of proportion to streamline the many charts and questionnaires.

I am also thankful to the many professional interviewers from business and industry who gracefully participated in my experiments and to those among them who patiently answered all of my questions and volunteered further information about their activities. I am particularly indebted to Mr. Kenneth Brewer, formerly with Service Merchandise Company in Nashville, Tennessee, and presently Director of Recruitment Training with National Bank and Trust in Oklahoma City, Oklahoma.

A sabbatical leave from Vanderbilt University made the time available to write up the data I had collected so that they could appear in book form. No other funding was provided by the University.

Although the book is written for a specialized audience of linguists, psychologists, semioticians, and communicationalists, it is hoped that it may help some young people to better prepare for that traumatic experience which is the first job interview.

Nashville, Tennessee
December 20, 1982

Walburga von Raffler-Engel
Professor of Linguistics

0. INTRODUCTION

Research into the perception of nonverbal behavior is fraught with an array of complications that are usually left unrecognized. The problems inherent in such research are of four kinds: legal, technical, systematic, and analytical.

The legal problems are tied to ethical consideration, at least in the opinion of this writer. There are many ways to circumvent the investigator's legal obligations towards his subjects in countries which have laws to protect an individual's privacy, and there are many countries where such laws either do not exist at all or are very lenient. I personally adhere to the legal obligations which bind researchers in the United States of America. Covert videotaping is permitted in open public spaces, such as streets and parks. Informed consent is required in private areas where individuals do not expect to be in the public view. This leaves several gray areas, such as cinemas, restaurants, and college classrooms. In cinemas and restaurants where I have done research, I have secured the permission of the respective manager. In classrooms I found it easy to obtain permission from the students but in many cases the instructor did not grant such permission making the taping impossible. Videotaping of minors involves parental consent and for children starting at age seven the additional consent by the child is also required. The researcher has to secure permission to tape, and to utilize the results for scholarly dissemination. If the latter involves showing the tapes or pictures thereof to third parties, the subjects have to grant authorization even when their names will be kept anonymous.

How much a subject's knowledge of being videotaped interferes with his normal behavior is hard to determine. Children tend to become hams but after a while forget about the taping equipment. Many adults seem to be totally unconcerned about the video machine, especially if they are promised that they may see the tape and erase any part on it which they find objectionable. A minority of adults need long and patient hours of taping before they can overcome their self-consciousness. The latter causes some to become so timid that they undergesticulate almost to the point of freezing while others overgesticulate abrasively. Still others become so nervous that they fidget and overuse self- and object-manipulators. It is always advisable to observe one's subjects during a lengthy get-acquainted period and possibly make sketches of them from memory after the sessions are finished in order to determine how much the taping influences their behavior.

For the topic of this book I have selected the career interview. Job applicants expect to be taped and interviewers find nothing unusual in having to fill out evaluative questionnaires. Overt videotaping thus does not violate the naturalness condition and the use of judges is not an artificial procedure.

The technical problems are only to a very limited extent inherent in the mechanical equipment, the latter being only a question of the availability of the financial resources and the technical expertise of the researcher. Of course, recording devices are constantly improving but when funding is limited, I would at least insist on the use of clean new tape. Whenever possible, I try to hire an experienced professional TV technician. It is not easy to organize the shooting and perform it at the same time, especially if the researcher is not particularly gifted in mechanics. The real difficulty is in covering the entire area while focusing on each subject in an identical manner as foregrounding and backgrounding tends to influence perception in subtle ways beyond the obvious factors of clarity and size of visibility. Even more vital is controlling the time of exposure. The gesture of a subject seen briefly adjusting his eye glasses will be barely noticed while the same subject repeatedly touching these same frames over a period of time appears to be nervous. Most importantly, the perception of an interactant varies depending on whether the applicant is seen alone or together with his conversation partner (von Raffler-Engel and McKnight 1981).

The above shows clearly how closely the technical aspects of taping intertwine with the systematic layout of the research design. The most difficult feature in most research designs, and more so when investigating nonverbal behavior, is not so much the isolation of the independent variable as the identification of the myriads of dependent variables. Some researchers accurately control for their subjects but fail to be as careful with their raters. In the hope of minimalizing the uncertainties that derive from these difficulties I have attempted a new approach to the design construction. Instead of using one design with a large number of subjects I have utilized a variety of research designs with a moderate number of subjects. This procedure I have called the multiple design approach. As noted by Bochner (1982: 22), Campbell and Fiske (1959) pointed out that it is desirable to approach a problem from many directions. Bochner (1982: 22) also draws attention to the multiple corroboration (a term used by Lykken (1968)) by which the results become more certain when the data from various approaches show a consistent pattern.

The complexities of the analytical procedure selected to determine the research results are particularly vexing in nonverbal studies because there is no consensus among specialists as to what constitutes a unit of nonverbal behavior. Even though I do not believe that the linguistically based structuralist position is necessarily irreconcilable with the more psychologically oriented external variable approach (von Raffler-Engel 1978), a clear idea of the nonverbal primes is still in the offing. My own definitions are operational and based on ad hoc entities which I keep constant throughout my research projects. Basically, I believe that Ekman's (1980) categorization comes closest to how the various modes of nonverbal behavior are perceived by the recipients. Although in reality they are not always neatly separated, within this analytical framework, one can distinguish three basic functions in communication, the referential, the regulatory, and the affective.

The *referential* function is sometimes called informative because it conveys the experiential message, such as the statement *There was a winding staircase* and the appropriate gesture of a twisting hand movement.

The *regulatory* function signals to the hearer that one is not quite finished talking by filling a pause with *uh* or *well* and/or bydirecting eye gaze away from the hearer (in societies like the North American where one looks at the inter-actant when listening and does so much less when speaking) and/or by increasing one's gesticulation. The hearer may nod slightly to signal that he wishes the speaker to go on, or he may nod strongly to point out that by now he intends to claim the speaking turn for himself.

The *affective* function relates to emotion. It regulates the total interactional relationship rather than it specifies. One may speak more 'kindly' to a child and 'harsher' to an insubordinate employee; or one may scratch one's head in front of a close friend but never in front of a recent acquaintance. The affective function is closely related to the regulatory function. A change in posture from relaxed to rigid symbolizes a metaphorical switch signalling to the conversational inter-actant that the introductory remarks are finished and that it is now time for the formal business transaction. In this function also pertain *self-manipulators* when an individual wrings his hands or nervously twirls his pencil. It is often next to impossible to determine whether the nervousness is induced by the content or style of the interaction or whether it is due to a previous ego-state. We cannot not communicate but not all behavior is communicative either in intent or in perception.

All three functions are message-related and in the study of nonverbal behavior their expressions should be classified under *kinesics*. Kinesics is to be distinguished from *body language*, or *action movements*. The latter are not pur-

posely interactional albeit there are areas of overlapping in both form and meaning. The distinction I draw is similar to the one made by Morris (1977:24-25)
between *Primary gestures* and *Incidental gestures.*

   Body language refers to movements of the body which are culture-specific
just as kinesic movements but carry no message beyond signalling an ego-state.
The manner in which people walk, hold their hands while smoking a cigarette,
or cross their legs differs greatly across cultures and between the sexes within
cultures. The following example may explain the line of demarcation between
body language and kinesics. A school principal calls two boys to his office and
eventually the boys agree that they will no more disrupt the class with their violent
behavior. When they are dismissed by the principal they walk away 'in a defiant
manner'. Here their style of walking had become kinesic informing the principal
of their true intentions. The defiant walking style may have been unconscious
but more likely was intentional. In any case, it was interpreted as such by the
principal who asked the boys to come back and 'walk away right' (von Raffler-
Engel 1980a).

   Linguists have devoted little, if any, attention to the perception of the
message. Discussions of the mirror theory of speech perception have not generally dealt with personality problems. Discussions of analysis by synthesis have
also ignored personality differences between speaker and hearer. Linguistic
research and linguistic theory have by and large not made substantive contribu-
tions to our understanding of the potential differences between intended and
perceived meaning.

   Linguists, like some philosophers, do not extend the concept of truth condition beyond the physical reality which can be verified on a superficial level.
Mathematical models by design do not deal with nongrammatical matters.
Pragmatics is infinitely more complex. Even those linguists that did not accept
the concept of the 'ideal speaker-hearer' have done little research into personality
differences between the hearer and the speaker beyond the social factors due to
cultural differences.

   In addition, our understanding of the perception of the message has been
hampered by the fact that in general, spoken language was analyzed as if it were
written language ignoring the fundamental difference between the two modes of
expression. In face-to-face interaction the message is conveyed verbally and nonverbally. The verbal component is only one part of the communication to be
supplemented by the nonverbal component. Theories about language were
developed that were much too powerful because they attributed to the verbal
component that which legitimately belongs to it plus additional features that are

non-existent in real life spoken language, belonging instead to the nonverbal component.

The importance of the nonverbal component in providing the full impact of the communicative event is always part of our unconscious reaction. It reaches our consciousness to varying degrees. One instance where the perception of nonverbal behavior is at its most fully conscious degree is during the career interview. Manuals for interviewers and evaluation sheets even codify certain specific types of nonverbal behavior.

Another persistent misconception and which is found even among people in communication is that a fixed ratio obtains between how much of the message is conveyed verbally and how much nonverbally. The term nonverbal is understood as the combination of all those elements, paralinguistic and kinesic, which are not part of the codified standard language. The misconception that a fixed ratio exists between verbal and nonverbal communication probably dates from an article by Mehrabian (1968) in a popular magazine. Unsophisticated readers misunderstood that he was talking about feelings and not about the total message. From this came a chain of statements, one copying from the other, that only 7% of a message is conveyed verbally. Mehrabian's observation that responsiveness to nonverbal cues may vary depending on social class was also lost in the process. Popular writing and speaking requires absolute figures and authors and lecturers usually settle for a ratio of 15% verbal to 85% nonverbal.

Most laymen believe that for speakers of the same language it would be easily possible to compile a dictionary of body movements in which each gesture, facial expression, or postural stance can be described by attributing to it a clearly defined single meaning. Some of the popular books on body language appear to foster such a concept of context-free kinesics. Such simpleminded approaches, at the most, are willing to consider the gesture cluster in which the meaning of a particular body configuration is affected by the simultaneous combination with other body configurations.

Goffman's many insights notwithstanding, among kinesicists, an area that has been largely disregarded is the social dimension of nonverbal behavior. The student of nonverbal behavior must take into account the entire interactional context and look at the quality of a body motion, its intensity, and its frequency. In protracted eye contact between individuals, there is a difference between a loving eye gaze and the hate stare. It is essential not to interpret gestures in isolation from each other and from the expression of the face. What determines the meaning is the gesture cluster, the combination of the various body motions produced together. A raised hand with a smile signifies a jest whereas a raised hand with an expression of anger must be taken as a threat.

Behavior in the dyad has been extensively researched in the past and it has been tacitly assumed that the findings could be transferred to group situations. This is not so. For one entire semester my students and I investigated the college classroom situation and we found that the rules governing the multi-faceted interaction of people in a group are not quite the same as those governing the speaking turn system in face-to-face interaction in the dyad (von Raffler-Engel and students 1979). The only study in existence so far that analyzes the synchronous multi-party interaction by one individual is my analysis of the Phil Donahue talk show (von Raffler-Engel 1982).

Little attention has generally been paid to differences in evaluating identical body movements by persons of diverse background. I constructed a series of research projects to find out about such variation in interpretation. The results showed differences in raters' sex and cultural and professional background to be statistically significant in determining judgment about certain types of kinesic behavior.

What I discovered was, first of all, that people have selective perception of body motions. We showed videotapes of a conversational interaction of medium kinesic style to persons from various cultures. The persons from high-kinesic cultures, such as South Americans, recalled almost all of the movements while the viewers from low-kinesic cultures, such as Britishers, had hardly noticed the presence of these movements (von Raffler-Engel et al. 1978). It is not yet clear to me whether the lack of recall would imply that the movement was not perceived at all or that it was only dimly perceived, or vaguely perceived, or even perceived in its entirety but not stored in the intermediate or long term memory. Once the image has been perceived in a selective manner, it has to be processed by the mind. Cognition also is determined by previous experience. In our research men and women with identical backgrounds were shown videotapes but their interpretation differed according to their sex. People from different professions also gave different interpretations of identical nonverbal behavior they had viewed on videotape (von Raffler-Engel and Gantz 1980).

The social setting in which face-to-face interaction takes place still needs considerable exploring. Works that provide information on nonverbal behavior in specific social settings rarely go beyond describing the meaning of a number of body motions which occur in that particular setting. These studies fulfill a useful function albeit they generally take the setting for granted. These settings lacking adequate description, it is not possible to isolate variables and replicate the experiments changing one variable at a time. Variation in form in the same type of basic human behavior, such as greeting rituals, has been researched by anthropologists but little is known about intra-cultural variation depending on the social situation.

What the student of nonverbal behavior misses most in current research is a framework for a macro-system to connect knowledge already available on micro-events and also to show how certain body movements are interpreted in one social setting against the interpretation of the same, or similar movement, in another social setting. Just like verbal language, kinesics lends itself to cross-cultural misunderstandings. These are of three types, misinterpretations, failures to notice, and overinterpretations. The first type is the one best known and the easiest to overcome. Sooner or later Americans will figure out that Europeans include the thumb in showing numbers with the hands, and that many Africans indicate the past (the known) by pointing to the front of their eyes while the future (the unknown) lies behind visibility. Errors of omissions are more subtle. Traditional Japanese consider it bad manners if one does not cover one's mouth while showing the teeth to bite into some ill-prepared food. This can be learned. The most troublesome are the errors of commission. Southern Italians may touch their earlobes to indicate that somebody is homosexual and a lady not familiar with this signal may cause somebody to attribute a meaning to her touching her earlobe, sore from a tight earclip, which she never intended to convey.

This book presents a common social situation in everyday life in the United States and analyzes the nonverbal behavior of the participants as they react differently, depending on their age, their sex, their profession, and possibly the degree of their personal involvement.

Throughout the book the term nonverbal is used in its restricted sense of pertaining to the appearance of the human body. Communication obtains on three levels. The first and best known level is that of language, also called the verbal level. Within the same channel of oral articulation is the level of paralanguage, also called vocal-nonverbal. The third level operates on a different channel, through motions of the body. It is called kinesics or nonverbal proper. A very clear schematization of interpersonal communication is available in Hulbert and Capon's (1972) brief survey.

Most researchers contrast language with paralanguage and kinesics. They emphasize the fact that language serves primarily the referential function of communication while both paralanguage and kinesics mainly serve the regulatory function. They also believe that the brain stores language in the left hemisphere and paralanguage and kinesics in the right part.

I have taken exception to the common practice considering the vocal-auditory channel as one biological unit which combines language and paralanguage. In contrast to it is the visual channel. I do not only insist on the different physiological modalities. More importantly, I believe that a clear-cut separation of language and paralanguage is impossible. This being the case, the assignment of the gray areas to either the verbal or the nonverbal level becomes a grave problem. I also conjecture that eventually we will discover that paralanguage is an integral part of language, or, rather, that paralanguage is only a temporary working term until we have fully analyzed the vocal channel in its entirety and gained a more complete understanding of how referential and regulatory meanings are conveyed and received. Body motions send both referential and regulatory signals. Deictic pointing and the affirmative head nod are referential signals. At this date brain research is not conclusive. Dividing the analysis of communicative behavior into its overt physiological channels has the advantage that it does not imply any value judgment. It being a descriptive rather than an interpretative decision, the findings from my research can be utilized from different theoretical perspectives. They are not contaminated by an evaluative decision to begin with.

I am limiting my research to kinesics exclusive of facial expression. This, I admit, is a severe limitation. There is only so much one can do, and I try to do what I can do best, leaving it to specialists in facial mimicry to cover that part eventually. I am not only less knowledgeable about the face than about the body, I am also less attracted to its study because so much more is known about the face already than is known about the body.

The research presented in this book, in conclusion, deals with the perception of the human body as it functions in the conversational face-to-face interaction. Beyond the motions of the body, posture, gesture, eye movement, spatial orientation and touch, I have included static forms of personal appearance, like body shape, sex, racial traits and clothing.

1. THE BUSINESS TRANSACTION

This book looks into nonverbal behavior in the face-to-face interaction within the business context. The social setting of the business transaction determines the content, the goal, and the means of the interaction. Throughout this book the term *business* will be used in its common sense meaning, which differs from the linguistic term 'business transaction' used in discourse analysis (see Edmondson 1981: 76) for any conversation which results in an alteration of the behavior of the interactants.

Business involves the transfer of money. Money is exchanged either for other forms of money, like securities, or for goods, such as real estate, or for services, as when a university hires a professor. The transaction could also involve simple barter where no money is physically involved. Money is always present, nevertheless, as the value of the items bartered is generally measured against its current monetary value rather than against the usefulness or the sentimental value of the items bartered as the sole criterion for their worth in the exchange. The concept of monetary value and the presence of an exchange mark the content of the business transaction. Money is also the key factor in contracting for services. The compensation for the service may take the form of an employee's salary or any other form. It is directly related to the need for such a service on the part of the employer and that need is conditioned by the return the latter expects from said service in direct or indirect revenue. As money ultimately represents the livelihood of both parties in the transaction, the career interview is a most serious interaction. Third parties who observe such a transaction are quite aware of this and should therefore be more alert and capable of keener judgments than when asked to rate most other types of experimental situations.

The goal of the business interaction is to bring to fruition an exchange of goods or services and this purpose is clear and known to the parties concerned. What makes the business transaction unique is not that it has a purpose. Language being a servo-mechanism, virtually all communicative interactions do have a purpose. By stating that its purpose is well defined, we narrow it down some but not sufficiently. In seduction the purpose is also quite clear to one party, but not necessarily is the other party fully aware of it. In the business transaction both parties know what they want and are cognizant of their reciprocal awareness.

Coercion not lying within legal business practices the goal must be pursued through persuasion. Psychologists and psychiatrists distinguish between persuasion and suggestion in the context of psychotherapy. Suggestion is a process of communication which causes change without critical judgment while persuasion influences through rational means. The distinction has its usefulness, but in my opinion it is not really a dichotomy. I prefer to view persuasion and suggestion as extremes on a scale which leads from magic to suggestion to persuasion. Persuasive discourse broadly defined is a communicative act intent at changing other's opinion or patterns of behavior by influencing one's judgment. The degree of rationality used by the persuader is not necessarily in direct relation to the rationality of the response on the part of the hearer. On the part of the speaker frequently the intentionality of suggestion is not on his conscious level. Depending on expertise and on self-awareness, the use of nonverbal behavior in persuading techniques runs the gamut from ignorance to manipulation. In the low-kinesic verbally oriented society of mainstream America, the perception of regulatory nonverbal behavior is to a large extent suggestive rather than rationally analyzed except for the highly trained observer. I doubt that any businessman ever engages in persuasion without suggestion, whatever his state of awareness and degree of intentionality.

If one wanted to schematize the major components of the face-to-face interaction in the business situation, the following outline would emerge:

Content
(1) involvement of money
(2) exchange of goods or services
Goal
(3) clearly defined purpose
(4) reciprocal awareness of purpose
Means
(5) persuasion
(6) suggestion

The discourse used in the job interview is a special sub-type of sales discourse. It differs from the more common types of sales discourse in that the item for sale is not a third entity, such as an object or a football player, but one of the transactants themselves. A further complexity arises in that the seller may find it difficult to engage in an active role. The lead belongs very definitely to the buyer and not to the person who does the selling. The interviewer who is the potential buyer initiates the questions and sets the tone for the interaction in a much more obvious way than in any other business transaction.

All conversational interactions generally follow a sequence of three stages, speech preparatory, speech central, and speech final (Jones and von Raffler-Engel 1981). In the first stage the two parties basically feel each other out. While in the career interview 'feeling each other out' is the purpose of the entire meeting even though this evaluatory process is structured within the normal three stage sequence. I will go into detail when I describe the interviewing process later in the book.

In the business transaction the nonverbal element looms extremely large. The two aspects of the sales transaction were researched by our group. The analysis of the buying process (Weisberg and von Raffler-Engel 1980) showed that if one listened to an audio recording of the verbal exchange between a salesman and his customer, understanding what they were talking about remained too vague to make much sense. "I need one about this size." – "The color should go well with this sample of my wallpaper." – "The one over there seems just right for you." The analysis of the paying process (Jones and von Raffler-Engel 1982) showed that it was a nonverbal cue which signalled to the store employee when the customer was ready to finalize his purchase.

2. THE CAREER INTERVIEW

The impact of nonverbal behavior is even more pronounced in the career interview. If during the sales transaction nonverbal cues complement and even supplement verbal cues, during the job interview the interpretation of nonverbal behavior becomes the primary goal. That personality is rated mostly on nonverbal cues is recognized in common language by expressions such as *I am going to look him over.*

Personality factors play a major role in any business transaction. Witness the many jokes about used car dealers. The buyer must have confidence in the reliability of the people that produce the product and the salesmen who merchandise it. The seller must have confidence in the fiscal solvency of the buyer. In the job interview more is at stake than credibility. Personality becomes the focus of the transaction. Most frequently it is the interviewer who examines the applicant, but in areas where the labor market is very strong, it is a two way process. When a candidate is particularly sought after the dominance relationship is reversed. This happens most often with openings in the highest ranks, like when a firm tries to hire a vice-president from a competitor. In addition to the general elements present in the business context, the interview situation encompasses the following elements:

Dyadic relationship	*Personality rating*
(7) one way dominance	(8) one way examination
or	or
shared dominance	reciprocal examination

For the student of nonverbal behavior the study of the career interview is an area of enormous potential and it is surprising that it has hardly been explored at all. Its study is interesting not only for a better understanding of face-to-face interaction per se. It has also very important historical implications for students of social change.

From the desiderata of the perfect interviewee that emerged from the data which I collected between 1978 and 1982, it is apparent that he is not the typical WASP stereotype. He is not the reserved man in the gray flannel suit. He may equally well be a woman or black. He looks like a person in livened-up banker's gray with just a touch of Latino gesticulation. The interpersonal space between the interviewer and the candidate too is midway between the Anglo and the Chicano extremes. The needs of the business community have drastically changed over the past decade. It is becoming clear to business schools that rather than train staff experts and functional specialists they have to produce managers that are prepared for "the crucial task of making decisions" (Bok 1981). To foster the capability for making crucial decisions, the previous teaching methods have given way to the Socratic technique of classroom discussions. The teaching method is directly related to the desired results, replacing the static defender of the status quo with a more articulate agent of change.

For the student of nonverbal behavior the correlation of instructional methods and goals is most intriguing. It bears on the controversy of whether the emotion triggers the expression or whether the physical expression generates the corresponding emotion. What is becoming ever more evident is that perseverance in an expressive configuration will increase the degree of the emotion thus represented. Approaches to mental health, such as dance therapy, have demonstrated that inducing certain body motions in an individual directly affects that person's state of mind. Professors in management schools and hiring officials in various businesses may not be interested in the theories underlying these findings but are intuitively aware of the relationship between expressive behavior and mental attitudes. Hiring officials are looking for individuals which show through their bodies that they have the intellectual power and the physical stamina to meet the needs of today's business community.

Interviewees are divided into two groups and their nonverbal behavior is judged from a different vantage point depending on whether the person to be evaluated is novel to the job market or has held previous appointments. Employers tell me that it requires far more expertise and time to judge the potential of a young person entering the profession than to judge the fit of an experienced person. Firms use different interviewers for campus recruiting than those they use for the recruitment of seasoned professionals. In both instances the interviewer judges the applicant on three scores:

(a) Can he do the job?
(b) Will he do the job?
(c) Can he get along with people?

The first of the three fundamental requirements is largely answered from the resumé. The college senior or recent MBA has provided the list of courses taken and grades received, letters of recommendation and, where applicable, full-

or part-time employment record. The professional who wants to change jobs has provided a list of his working experience and names of references. During the interview the truthfulness of the information may be verified. While talking about the matter, the interviewer watches for signs of nervousness, a quivering voice, loss of eye contact or an embarrassed facial expression, and fidgeting in posture and hands. The verification of the candidate's credentials can be done before the interview and is not always part of the interview itself. What is always done in answer to the first question is observing whether the candidate could perform the particular job the interviewer has in mind and do so within the requirements of the particular firm to which he is applying.

The answer to the first question involves two types of judged capability. One is directly related to the technical fulfillment of the job requirements. An insurance company, for example, will expect a salesman to be free of any nervous tics, speak forcefully and present an overall impression of authority coupled with honesty. An accountant to work in an office might as well be a quiet type, and if he is otherwise highly qualified it does not matter too much if he scratches his nose. The second type of capability is more specifically related to the applicant's personality. Can he withstand pressure? The interviewer checks the applicant's bodily reaction to a sudden silence, a probing personal question at the limits of the legality of such questions. Does the applicant show 'enthusiasm' when he talks about his past work, his future projects? That is, do his eyes shine, does his torso straighten? If he shows no drive he is not easily promotable and enployees that do not advance get disgruntled.

The second fundamental question concerns whether the applicant is willing to do his job. Absentee rates are generally verified before the interview albeit this cannot be done for college students without a previous employment record. The presence or absence of a positive attitude towards accepting orders combined with the leadership capacity to take the initiative have to be explored through the candidate's verbal and nonverbal behavior. Does he show polite manners? Does the direction of his seating posture indicate aggressiveness without abrasiveness?

The third question, like the first one, is rated on different scores depending on the opening for which the candidate is being considered. Nobody hires a person who cannot get along with people. The degree, however, to which such congeniality is required varies with the job. A draftsman who has to share the office with others or a computer programmer in a university who has to work closely with the faculty will have to be more adaptable to other people than a translator who works from his home. For certain jobs, like public relations officer or receptionist, getting along with people, beyond a personality requirement, becomes an absolute part of the job qualifications. In the dyad of the ongoing interview session the candidate is probed for courtesy, friendliness and primarily on whether he can establish rapport. The latter is evaluated by interviewers on a 'gut feeling'. I asked several interviewers to define what they meant by this and nobody came up with more than that interviewing is an art rather than a science, that "you just get a feeling", that he is "experienced in sizing up people", that he tries to "establish rapport with the candidate". Kinesicists, of course, do describe the nonverbal manifestation of 'rapport'. It is interactional synchrony. During the interviews which were actually observed by my students and myself, we noticed that conversation partners established kinesic synchrony either in the mirror or parallel image. They frequently shared posture shifts, even smiled at each other, but especially noticeable were their legs getting into the bookending position. The ultimate test of the getting-along-with-people quality comes when the candidate is asked to go to the plant and meet with his peers, superiors, and inferiors socially in a group situation.

The whole purpose of the second interview is to test the candidate's ability to fit within the structure of the organization. Such fit was defined for me by interviewers as the candidate's potential for getting along with existing employees, and possibly his ability to lead, if the case may require it, without causing friction. For the second interview the candidate is flown to the place of his projected employment not only so that his future teammates can look him over and express their opinion of him but, mostly, so that the future employer can observe the candidate's interaction against the background of his projected place of work, how he would mesh with the firm and the community. Nonverbal behavior is the key factor.

Job applicants are by and large conscious of the fact that they are evaluated for personality traits besides work performance and this awareness structures their behavior during the interview. Applicants fall into two categories and, of course, all shades in between. Some applicants, especially the younger and less experienced ones, have preconceived ideas about how they should behave. Some college seniors even get the wrong advice. They sit still believing that these are 'good manners'. They answer questions but do not pose any themselves, and are so concerned about following the rules of propriety as they conceive them that they hardly pay any attention to the nonverbal behavior of the interviewer nor to his tone of voice. Worst of all, when these applicants do not get offers for second interviews, they become even more concerned with what they believe is adequate behavior and their chances for employment deteriorate increasingly with every new interview. Eventually, they fail to see how much importance the interviewer attributes to their actual behavior during their face-to-face interaction as compared to the content of their resumé. They also overemphasize the impact of their verbal expression in relation to the impression they convey nonverbally.

College seniors at their first attempt to get professional employment who have not been given any instruction or, worse, the wrong instructions, lessen their chances rather than improve them as they gain experience in being interviewed. The gap between what interviewers perceive as important and what applicants believe widens in most respects. These are the conclusions from a survey which my students, William Glasgow and Judy Olin, conducted at the Vanderbilt University Career Planning and Placement Services. Potential employers contact that office and the staff members then make available this information to college seniors who line up for interviews with the representatives of the firms for which their college background qualifies them. The University Placement Office provides the students' resumés to the potential employers who want to examine them. I am grateful to the director of the Vanderbilt University Career Planning and Placements Services, Mrs. Ava Sellers, for her generosity in allowing my researchers access to her facilities.

A questionnaire asking for identical information was given to ten interviewers selected at random and to fifty students that had no interviewing experience and fifty students who had experienced more than three interviews at the Vanderbilt Placement Office. The results are as follows: (The designs are by W. P. Glasgow.)

Key to Illustrations:

students with interview experience

students without interview experience

professional interviewers

I. Question: What emphasis do you feel the interviewer places on your appearance compared to your verbal expression?

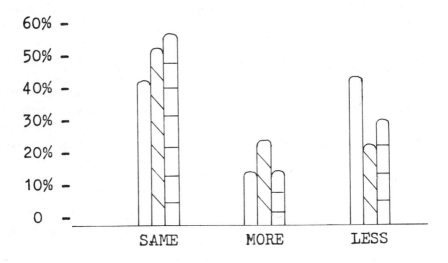

II. Question: What emphasis do you feel the interviewer places on your personal mannerisms compared to your verbal expression?
Answer: Weighs the same.

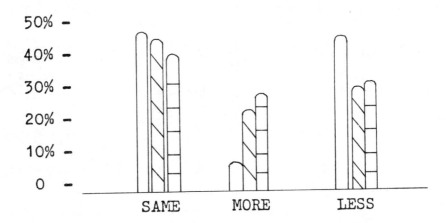

III. Question: How much emphasis do you feel is placed on eye contact?

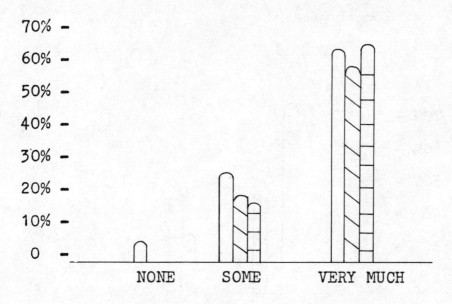

IV. Question: Do you think your posture is noticed?

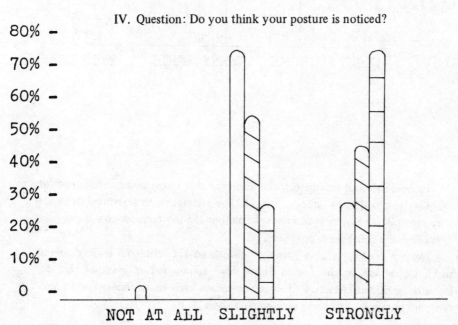

V. Question: How much importance do you think an interviewer attributes
to nervous fidgeting?

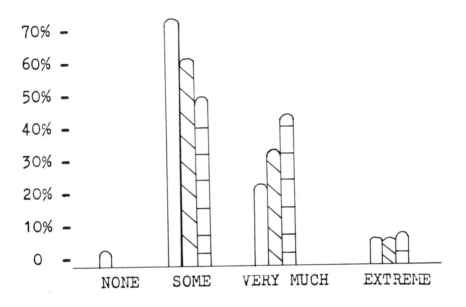

From a practical standpoint, the results of this survey point to the need for
adequate instruction to college students. For researchers in nonverbal behavior
they are indicative of how unaware people outside the business community are
of the changes that have taken place.

    Western society is at a turning point from the industrial society to the
technological age. In the United States news commentators speak of the 'de-
industrialization of America'. Job requirements have vastly changed and applicants are screened to fit these new prerequisites.

VI. Question: Do you think hand gesture will influence an interviewer's evaluation of you?

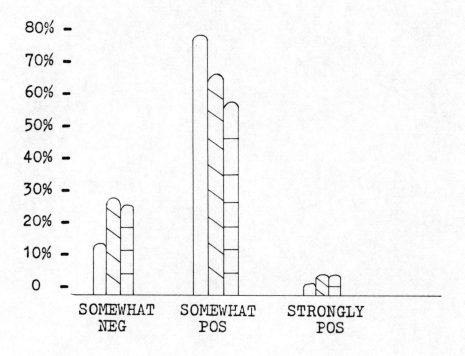

3. THE ACADEMIC INTERVIEW

Nowhere is the change in nonverbal behavior that occurred in the United States during the last decade more evident than in the Academic Interview. Most laymen and even most professors still believe that a scholarly sense of detachment is expected from them. Conversations with deans and department chairmen revealed that what may make or break an applicant for a teaching position in a college or university is precisely the opposite.

A typical interview goes as follows. The search committee has restricted the candidates to those that are competent and well-published. The interview thus does not check on these points at all. What the applicant has to demonstrate is that he is a superior teacher. Previous to the meeting, the interviewer reads only the abstracts and not the full publications of the candidate. This will enable him to ask probing questions and still be able to judge first hand whether the candidate's explanations are easily understood and generate further questions. He listens for clarity and enthusiasm. To check for classroom effectiveness the interviewer imagines himself to be a student. If the applicant does not start to make drawings on paper, the interviewer will hand him a yellow pad with the covert intent of simulating a blackboard situation. While all this speaking and writing goes on, the interviewer watches for distracting movements that would indicate nervousness. He also watches for forceful gesticulation which enhances the teacher's presentation. The posture should show eagerness. Very important is a sense of humor and the capability to cope with interferences, like removing the yellow pad before the candidate is finished. The interviewer may momentarily direct his gaze away from him to see whether the candidate has the power to redirect eye contact towards his interactant. At some point the interviewer will inquire about the breadth of the applicant's scholarly interests and watch for signs of excitement as this is a promise for future research. Nonverbal signs of excitement are said to be posture shifts, tensing of the body, and increased gesticulation. Clothing is not very important unless it is outlandish, which never really happens these days.

To observe how well the candidate would fit with his potential colleagues he has lunch with them and then there is a reception in the evening. A lecture delivered by the candidate the following morning is evaluated by both faculty and students.

In sum, the adacemic interview does not differ in any substantial manner from the business interview. The three basic areas of evaluation are the same. There is some difference in the evaluation of the first area — can he do the job? In business the applicant's expertise is rated almost entirely from his resumé and record of past experience, while in teaching a show of the actual performance of duties is required. Contrary to popular opinion, nonverbal behavior is even more important in the academic interview than in business, except show business. Decreasing enrollment has transformed a sedate profession into show business.

4. THE INTERACTIONAL ELEMENT

In the industrial society teamwork is not as overwhelmingly present as it is in the technological society. The symbol of the industrial age may be the assembly line where every worker is on his own in his monotonous task. The technological revolution is one of constant adaptation of pre-existing systems to new technologies. Productivity is not measured in numbers of output but in improvements. It is cooperative by definition. The third of the three main criteria on which an applicant is judged, whether he can get along with people, looms ever larger. Most interviewers and some interviewees realize that the evaluation involves the applicant's interactional behavior beyond the analysis of his basic personality features. The literature in nonverbal communication is rich in studies on interaction but what was needed was a comparison of the same behavior by an individual alone and when seen in interaction. This is what I prepared with my student Steven McKnight (von Raffler-Engel and McKnight 1981). The results clearly indicate that the perception of nonverbal behavior varies in function of the visible access to one or both of the interactants even with the clear contextual (and stated) understanding that the one end in view was participating in a dyadic conversation. The presentation of such an isolated end is quite naturalistic when the raters view a candidate being interviewed for a business position. In this particular situation it would not seem contrived that the camera had focused exclusively on the interviewee who was to be judged.

4.1. *Instrument*

Six white males of close range in age (the youngest being 22 and the oldest 26 years old), of similar physical build, and compatible education and socio-economic background were video taped in a mock business interview situation with the same interviewer, a white male in his late thirties. To preserve naturalness, each participant was instructed not to memorize the script but basically say the same things.

The following is the text for the interview which was handed to each participant as a model for what he was to say.

Interviewer: What made you decide to apply to our company?

Applicant: I am interested in management and I thought that working in a department store would offer the most varied exposure. Your company is very large and therefore should have many openings.

Int.: Do you know how our company is organized?

App: Yes, I researched it in Standard and Poor's.

Int.: That is fine. Would you mind telling me a little about yourself. What are your long- and short-range career goals? How will you go about obtaining them?

App.: My long-range goal is to become the vice-president of a company, and possibly even president. I enjoy organizational work and I do not mind long hours. I also would like to become free of financial worries and have a good life for myself and my family. I am certain that I will reach my goal by working hard, by listening to the advice of experienced people, and by conscientiously doing what is requested of me. I also plan to keep informed on new developments in my field through the trade journals. My short-term goal is to start at the bottom in a company that has a great reputation, like yours.

Int.: What is your weakest point?

App.: To tell the truth, I am a perfectionist. I always want to do everything to perfection and I might pay too much attention to details.

Int.: Are you capable of determining what is relevant and what is less essential in a task you are told to perform?

App.: Well, one of the things I learned in college was to analyze things critically and determine what is really important. Otherwise, I would have lost too much time studying for one course and got poor grades in the others due to a lack of time.

Int.: I'd like you to take a brief look at the brochure about our store on the table before we continue.

The verbal behavior of the applicants was virtually identical in language and content and varied as little as possible in paralanguage but their nonverbal behavior differed on one variable. The interviewer behaved in an identical manner throughout. Each taped session lasted three minutes.

The six interactions were taped on consecutive days and the interviewees had no occasion to meet at that time. Ideally I should have hired professional actors but this was financially out of the question. In regard to the nonverbal behavior to be portrayed by the student volunteers I opted for what I considered the minor evil. Instead of giving rigid instructions to each applicant so that they all would behave in an almost identical manner except for the one variable which we wanted to isolate, I simply told them to behave naturally except for one specific nonverbal manifestation which they were to stress without overdoing it to the point of caricature. In this manner I thought to avoid a stilted, artificial behavior throughout the tape. From past experience in nonverbal testing I am fairly certain that the dependent variables which might compound the picture would be of minor concern given the overriding effect of the independent variable (von Raffler-Engel 1980b).

The variations in nonverbal behavior are as follows. The six video frames were shown in the order listed below with one minute intervals between each frame to allow for rating time.

(I)   *Overgesticulation.* The applicant gesticulated almost constantly with his hands while he talked. The movements were appropriate but lacked the usual pauses.

(II) *Lack of adequate eye contact.* The applicant only rarely established eye contact with the interviewer, looking 'in the air' (as described by one observer) or downward.

(III) *Moderate aggressiveness.* The applicant did all the 'right' things (for a list of these see von Raffler-Engel 1980) but without forcefulness.

(IV) *Kinesic stillness.* The applicant kept his body still except for occasional head nods and some small movements with his fingers.

(V)   *Fidgeting.* The applicant fidgeted nervously, used frequent self-adaptors and played with the elastic band of his wrist watch.

(VI) *Positive aggressiveness.* The applicant did all the 'right' things but with great forcefulness in the tensing of his body and the intensity of his gaze.

4.2. Subjects

A total of 78 judges evaluated the tapes. Of these 42 were undergraduate students (M 21/F 21) and 36 were professionals (M 19/F 17) ranging in age from 23 to 68, mean 38.5 years. These professional raters were managers in department stores and admissions officers in the graduate professional schools of Vanderbilt University.

The subjects were classified into four categories: student males, student females, professional males, and professional females. Each category was then randomly divided. Half of the raters saw the applicant and the interviewer on the screen while the other half saw only the applicant. The two versions of the tape had been prepared at the Vanderbilt University Learning Resources Center by using two cameras. One camera focused on the two interactants while the other camera covered only the applicant. In this manner the applicant alone is slightly larger than when he is seated across the office table with the interviewer. Whether the difference in size had any influence on the evaluation of his behavior I cannot know as I did not run a small test comparing two identical pictures varying only in size.

The subjects viewed the tape singly or in small homogeneous groups. The students saw it in regular classrooms. The professionals viewed the tape at their place of work. (For my student this frequently meant carrying the heavy portable video equipment all over Nashville, Tenn.) Each judge filled out a demographic data sheet indicating sex, age, and years of experience in interviewing (see Appendix I). After viewing each of the six frames the judges compiled a forced-choice rating sheet evaluating the applicant on a set of personality and job related traits, and indicating whether he or she would hire/not hire him with/ without reservations. (See Appendix II)

4.3. *Analysis*

The test results were analyzed separately for each of the four subject categories, and for the students and the professionals as a whole as well as for all the women compared to all the men. The individual responses on the rating sheets were totalled for each question and comparisons were established on a percentile basis. See sample statistical chart on the opposite page:

4.4. *Results*

The results suggest the following typology in regard to nonverbal behavior when observed in an individual with or without the benefit of visual access to the other interactant.

4.4.1. *Non-interactional behavior.*

Behavior that is basically unrelated to the verbal behavior, or any other aspect of the ongoing conversational interaction. This behavior simply denotes an ego-state and has no direct interactional function.

An example of this type is the fidgeting applicant. It is exclusively in reference to his intelligence that differences in ratings appear. When he is alone, 91% of the male students consider him of average intelligence while when seen with his interactant that figure shrinks to 70%. When he is alone, no male student (0%) considers him below average, while in interaction 30% give him such a

Professionals (n. 36)

OVERGESTICULATION

		-With interactant- (F9 M10)			-Alone (F8 M9)		
		Female	Male	Total	Female	Male	Total
1. a)	yes	56%-5	30%-3	42%-8	50%-4	44%-4	47%-8
	no	44%-4	70%-7	58%-11	50%-4	56%-5	53%-9
b) a)		0%	0%	0%	25%-1	25%-1	25%-2
b)		0%	0%	0%	25%-1	25% -1	25% -2
c)		100%-5	100%-3	100%-8	50%-2	50%-2	50%-4
2.	a)	11%-1	10%-1	11%-2	63%-5	22%-2	41%-7
	b)	89%-8	90%-9	89%-17	38%-3	78%-7	59%-10
	c)	0%	0%	0%	0%	0%	0%
3.	a)	22%-2	0%	11%-2	38%-3	44%-4	41%-7
	b)	22%-2	40%-4	32%-6	25%-2	11%-1	18%-3
	c)	56%-5	60%-6	58%-11	38%-3	44%-4	41%-7
4.	yes	78%-7	70%-7	74%-14	88%-7	67%-6	76%13
	no	22%-2	30%-3	26%-5	13%-1	33%-3	24%4
5.	a)	0%	0%	0%	38%-3	11%-1	24%4
	b)	100%-9	80%-8	89%-17	50%-4	89%-8	71%-12
	c)	0%	20%-2	11%-2	13%-1	0%	6%-1
6.	a)	0%	0%	0%	0%	0%	0%
	b)	33%-3	20%-2	26%-5	13%-1	33%-3	24%-4
	c)	0%	0%	0%	0%	0%	0%
	d)	33%-3	10%-1	21%-4	50%-4	33%-3	41%-7
	e)	33%-3	70%-7	53%-10	38%-3	33%-3	35%-6

low rating. Among male professionals the same holds true. When alone 60% consider him average and 33% below average while visibly in interaction the exact opposite is shown: 33% average and 60% below. Among female professionals there is virtually no difference in his intelligence rating in the two pictures. With female students, however, he gains by being with his interactant, 80% considering him of average intelligence and only 20% below. When he is alone, the reverse holds true, with 36% average and 64% below. On no other score is there significant rater variation for the two tapes.

4.4.2. Interactional behavior.

Behavior that is intimately related to the face-to-face interaction. Interactional behavior has two aspects. It is judged for the effectiveness of its referential functon and of its regulatory function.

A classic example of the referential function is the overgesticulator. When he is alone, it is evident that his active gesticulation corresponds exactly to what he says. Of those professionals who would hire him, 25% would do so enthusiastically, and 25% without reservations. When seen with the interactant, all those that would hire him would do so with reservations (100%). When alone, 41% of all professionals consider him of outstanding intelligence, while in interaction that percentage shrinks to 11%. When he is alone, 24% consider him highly competent, while nobody (0%) thinks this of him in interaction. The judges seem to notice a conflict between the self-priming value of gesticulation and the disturbing influence of one-sided overgesticulation on the harmony of conversational interaction. The disharmony is especially blatant because the interviewer was kinesically very quiet. Nobody (0%) wants him as a personal friend or boss. When seen alone, 41% might take him as an employee but only 21% would do so after seeing him with his interactant.

The kinesically still applicant is the opposite of the overgesticulator. When viewed alone, no student (0%) and only 2 professionals (11%) think of him as outstandingly intelligent. 24% of the professionals even think of him as below average while when he is alone, he falls lower in intelligence and only 65% consider him average. Although unresponsively quiet, like all the others, this applicant establishes normal eye contact and therefore is moderately adequate in the regulatory function.

The applicant who gazes in the void may be considered self-reliant when seen alone by 35% of the professionals but only 11% think this of him when they see him in interaction. 65% consider him insecure when he is alone, and this figure jumps to 89% when the professionals see him in interaction.

The positively aggressive applicant is 100% successful in getting hired by the professionals on both tapes and only a single student would not hire him, and this only when he was seen alone. None of the professionals (0%) would want him as a personal friend when they see him alone but when they see him in interaction 26% would want him as a friend. When viewed alone, only his forcefulness stood out. When his behavior contrasted with the reserved personality of the interviewer, it took on a dimension of dominance improper for the particular social situation.

The moderately aggressive applicant also gets himself hired by all the professionals and only two students would not hire him, but this time it is when they see him in interaction. No female student would want him as a personal friend after seeing him alone but 40% want him as their friend when they see him in interaction. When seen alone his behavior did not manifest any degree of inappropriate dominance.

4.5. Conclusion

The intended meaning of the various applicants' behavior is evidently one and only one on both tapes. Observers' perception of many of these behaviors, however, changed depending on whether the applicant was viewed alone or within his full interactional context. The applicant on the tape and the raters shared the same culture and kinesic expectancies. The raters knew that there was another member to the interaction even when he was not visibly on the screen. Physically seeing or not seeing him, however, greatly influenced their perception of the interactant to be judged. The visual image guided rater imagination to emphasis on the referential function when the visual stimulus towards the regulatory function was not present. Hearing the questions to which the applicant replied and having consciousness of the fact that there was an interviewer in the actual event was not sufficient condition for an equal evaluation of both functions. One is reminded of theories in sociolinguistics, where the perceiver is part of the perceived.

5. HIERARCHICAL EVALUATION OF NONVERBAL BEHAVIORS

There is no question that the evaluation of job applicants is extensively based on the latter's nonverbal behavior during the interview.

So far, I had some idea on what type of nonverbal behavior was acceptable in a job interview and what type was not, but I had no clear guidelines to classify such behaviors hierarchically either singly or in combination. A literature search revealed that no such classification had yet been achieved at the time of my research (Fall 1978). McGovern and Ideus (1978) had tested low-kinesic and high-kinesic behavior in job applicants and found that rather motionless candidates received consistently negative ratings. No research established a more specified hierarchy.

In order to determine the possible hierarchy of various body motions in this evaluative process I used two very different approaches, one written and closed-ended, and one oral and open-ended. The results from these two testing procedures reinforced each other and I am therefore confident that my findings are valid. The hierarchical grouping of nonverbal manifestations was one of the earliest questions that came to mind, in 1978, when I initiated my research on the career interview. It is still part of an ongoing project to find further types of behavior and possibly establish gesture clusters of varying polarity.

To begin with, I designed a forced-choice questionnaire for a survey which was conducted by one of my ablest students, Elizabeth B. Battey.

The subjects were 30 corporate campus recruiters, twenty-four males and six females. They had come to the Vanderbilt Career Planning and Placement Service from all over the United States to interview seniors for positions within their companies. The 30 subjects had been randomly selected by the director of the Career and Placement Service as time permitted.

The questionnaire was divided into two parts. The first part contained the personal data, the interviewer's age, sex, level of education, the name of the company he represented, his position within the company and how much experience he had in interviewing. The second part represented the questionnaire proper aimed at revealing how much certain manifestations of nonverbal behavior affected the interviewer. These manifestations include the applicant's general appearance, posture, fidgeting, use of hands to gesticulate, maintenance of eye contact, and odor. There was space for comments following each question. The final question asked the interviewer to rank on a scale from 0 to 9 the amount that nonverbal behavior affected the applicant's skills and background.

The questionnaires were handed to the subjects at the Vanderbilt University Career Planning and Placement Service during slack periods between interviewing students. They filled them out in about fifteen minutes each and handed them back to Battey.

Below is a sample of the actual questionnaire.

SURVEY QUESTIONNAIRE

COMPANY:

TYPES OF JOBS FOR WHICH INTERVIEWING:

INTERVIEWER:

Position or title: Level of education:
Sex: M —— F ——   High School ——
Age: College   ——
    20 to 30 years ——   Masters   ——
    30 to 40 years ——   Ph.D.   ——
    40 to 50 years ——
    50 to 60 years ——
    60 years or over ——

1) How much emphasis do you place on a person's general appearance?

         None   Some   Very Much   Extreme

What do you consider good general appearance?
What do you consider bad general appearance?

2) Do you notice a person's posture?

         None   Some   Very much   Extremely

What do you consider to be good posture?
What do you consider to be bad posture?

3) How much does it influence your evaluation of a person when he fidgets with his clothes, hair, or some other object?

> None   Some   Very much   Extremely

4) How does it influence your evaluation of a person when he uses his hands while talking?

> Positively   Negatively

How much does this influence your evaluation of him?

> None   Some   Very much   Extremely

5) How much does it influence your evaluation of a person when he fails to maintain eye contact as he talks with you?

> None   Some   Very much   Extremely

6) Have you ever noticed an odor on a person you interviewed? If so, how much does it affect your evaluation of the person?

> None   Some   Very much   Extremely

7) Overall, how much weight do you place on the above behaviors in comparison to a person's skills and background?

> 0   1   2   3   4   5   6   7   8   9

8) Do you have any other suggestions on behavior which is detrimental to a person during an interview?

9) How do you define your experience in interviewing? (Check any of the following which apply.)

—— Relatively inexperienced   —— Consistent interviewing

The data from the questionnaire were compiled by computer and analyzed by another student, Jeffrey J. Rothschild. A number was assigned to each answer. The last question was already ranked from (0) to (9). All other answers which indicated degree were ranked from (1) to (4). Any 'yes' answer was assigned a (1). Any 'no' answer was assigned a (2). Any 'male' interviewer was assigned a (1). Any 'female' interviewer was assigned a (2).

The mean and the median to each answer regarding the applicant's non-verbal manifestations were calculated. The means and the medians were ranked from highest to lowest in order to reveal which manifestations most influenced the interviewer's evaluation of the applicant.

Cross-tabulations employing Pearson's Correlation and Chi^2 were used to determine relationships among the variables to establish whether the interviewer's ranking of nonverbal manifestations correlated with characteristics of the interviewers. On the opposite page are the tabulated results.

After we had analyzed the results from the forced-choice rating sheet, Elizabeth Battey personally asked one third (n.10) of the respondents to specify what they understood by our categories. The most offensive odor does not come from stale breath but from clothing that has an alkaline smell of cheap soap. This was as much of a surprise to us as the fact that unpleasant odor ranks as the most unfavorable trait an applicant could have. Important to my subsequent research was to find out that the category 'gesticulation' was ambiguous as it combined illustrators (which are positive) with adaptors (which are negative) and this category should therefore be discarded from our statistics.

The general results of the survey revealed that at a negative hierarchy listing the most objectionable features in decreasing order can clearly be established. It goes from odor (mainly cheap soap), to lack of eye contact, to general appearance (a business suit is expected for the first interview and becomes imperative on the follow-up interview), to posture (a candidate must show determination: a slump is negative, and leaning forward towards the interviewer is positive). The use of hand gestures is judged favorably, particularly in regard to sales jobs which require 'forcefulness' (von Raffler-Engel 1980c).

The survey also disclosed inherent differences among male and female interviewers. I have consequently expanded on that issue and will report the findings later in chapter 10.

SURVEY RESULTS

NONVERBAL BEHAVIOR OF APPLICANTS RANKED
IN HIERARCHY OF IMPORTANCE BY INTERVIEWER
Population: 30 (24 M / 6 F)

Manifestation	Mean	Median
Odor	3.500	3.667
Eye Contact	3.233	3.269
General Appearance	2.900	2.935
Posture	2.633	2.676
Fidgeting	2.600	2.571
Use of hands	2.567	2.123

Variables	Pearson's R	Significance
Profess x Sporadic	-.64466	.0001
Profess x Eye Contact	-.30497	.0506
Sporadic x Eye Contact	.51256	.0019
Sex x Fidgeting	.46371	.0049
Sex x Eye Contact	.30274	.0520
Genap x Fidgeting	.32323	.0407
Genap x Eye Contact	.46320	.0050
Posture x Hands	.48148	.0047
Posture x Eye Contact	.30385	.0513
Fidgeting x Eye Contact	.39456	.0003
Hands x Odor	-.36177	.0293

Abbreviations

Profess-	an interviewer who labeled himself as a professional interviewer
Sporadic-	an interviewer who labeled himself as a sporadic interviewer
Sex-	the sex of an interviewer
Genap-	the importance of an applicant's general appearance to the interviewer
Posture-	the importance of an applicant's posture to the interviewer
Fidgeting-	the importance of an applicant's fidgeting to the interviewer
Hands-	the importance of an applicant's use of hands while talking
Eye Contact-	the importance of an applicant's eye contact to the interviewer
Odor-	the importance of an applicant's odor to the interviewer

6. INTERVIEWING THE INTERVIEWER

Questionnaires and tests are the standard means for gathering data. Administering tests and questionnaires is not extremely time consuming and forced-choice responses are easily computed. The results look neat and impressive and generally do not have too many gray areas that make interpretation difficult. Funding agencies look favorably upon them and so do editors of learned journals. Standard academic research rarely uncovers facts that open new avenues of knowledge. In the real world where decisions involve financial outlays that do not come from the taxpayer, a more cautious approach is needed.

Business firms before hiring an employee conduct live interviews. In a similar vein, my research project has two facets. One is the more conventional one of forced-choice questionnaires which, however, were supplemented with requests for open-ended comments. The second facet of the research project is more unconventional consisting of a series of semi-structured informal meetings with executives and recruiters from industrial firms and employment agencies over a period of two years. These meetings that lasted from one to over two hours were held with experienced business interviewers in Nashville, Tennessee, either in their office or in mine. The atmosphere was kept informal and only semi-structured in the sense that I had a set of questions in mind which my students and I planned to ask. These questions were not asked in a pre-set order but as the flow of the conversation required. The person from business was encouraged to volunteer any additional information he was willing to provide, and was free to spend as much or as little time as he wished on the questions that were pre-selected. The basic questions asked in the meetings were the same of the Hierarchy Survey Questionnaire described in the previous chapter, but the scope of these questions was expanded to deal specifically with women and minorities and the ways in which the evaluation of these might possibly differ compared to the standard white male applicant.

A total of 20 personnel specialists were interviewed in this manner, 16 were males: 15 white, 1 black; 4 were females: 3 white, 1 black. They were selected because of their availability. Some were met originally at the Vanderbilt Career Planning and Placement Service, some at the Meeting of the Industrial Personnel Association which will be mentioned later in connection with the Five

Categories Tape test, and some were personal friends of mine or introduced to me through friends. Five interviews were conducted by my student William Glasgow, who was my co-worker for more than two years, one by Gena McNeal and Tyler Harrison, and fourteen by myself. I owe particular gratitude to Mr. Kenneth Brewer, College Relations Director and Senior Management Information Systems Recruiter of Service Merchandise, who gave me a set of professional printed materials and in-house publications besides a considerable amount of valuable information, and to Mr. William Spiller, Employee Relations Manager for Aladdin Industries, who gave me a number of bibliographical references which I would never have found otherwise.

In order not to disrupt the leisurely atmosphere of the meetings nor slow down the normal conversation tempo, most meetings were recorded on a small audiotape. These tapes were later transcribed by Judy Olin who was one of my most active students throughout the project.

Subsequently, the typescripts, or handwritten notes of the meetings that had not been taped, were xeroxed and rearranged according to topics so that all information pertaining to a particular topic was available within the same paragraph. Irrelevant social remarks were deleted from the record.

Eventually a set of 8 x 5 cards was prepared and filed in alphabetical order with all the necessary cross-references. Each card was divided by a line in the middle. On the left half was indicated the *Manifestation* and on the right half its *Interpretation*. Lack of eye contact is a manifestation and it is interpreted as symptomatic of insecurity, disinterest, insincerity.

Under each manifestation is indicated the degree it plays in the hierarchy of negative or positive features with the various sources of information, such as the initials of the person who mentioned it during our personal meeting. Later on, the structured sources were added, such as the surveys and questionnaires.

A separate file was prepared for groups of interviewees, such as women, minorities, and older people. The cards in those files were adequately cross-referenced with each other.

6.1. *Literature search*

A computer search on the literature was conducted to supplement the material that had been suggested by some of the professional interviewers. All institutes that train interviewers that had come to my knowledge were contacted and their brochures and texts were collected. In addition to these printed materials, I secured as many industrial in-house materials and evaluation sheets as I could.

A good idea of what points are emphasized in the training of interviewers can be gained by perusing the table of contents of a classic like Fear's *Evaluation Interview* (1978).

All these sources were examined for data on the same categories which had been listed on the cards. A new card was prepared to be filed directly after each corresponding card in the already existing file and marked 'Secondary sources'. Each source was indicated in the same manner as on the cards with the primary data from my research. No new categories were discovered by going through the literature.

6.2. *Manifestation and interpretation*

The most rewarding insight I gained from meeting with the various hiring officials was a better understanding of what certain aspects of nonverbal behavior 'mean'. Although there was divergence in the importance interviewers attributed to certain behaviors in the evaluation of an applicant, they generally agreed on how they interpreted such behaviors. They had names for nonverbal behaviors which were foreign to me but terms could easily be matched. What was most intriguing were the many interpretations for which interviewers found it hard to describe the actual manifestation. Obviously, they had never stopped to analyze some gesture clusters. Their concern after all, was not descriptive but plainly applied. This does not mean that they were not concerned with theories. They were indeed and eager to talk about them. The theories related to ways for detecting which nonverbal manifestations correlated to any one of the three basic questions, to whether the applicant can and will do the job and whether he can get along with people. All three questions were evaluated in relation to the particular job for which the applicant was considered and/or the one he could eventually be requested to perform. My analysis of these conversations were in many ways more interesting than reading the standard literature on kinesics or on interactional behavior or general communication. I look forward to more of such informal meetings with people in all sorts of professions and capacities sometime in the future so that I may gain a greater understanding of how nonverbal expressions are really perceived. Persons outside the professions that evaluate people may be much more difficult to prod for information as their judgments will be much more unconscious. It is known that the study of labels for nonverbal actions gives insight into what is on the conscious or semiconscious level with a certain culture. To begin with, it would be advisable to collect such labels. Unfortunately, time did not permit me to prepare a list of labels for the job interview situation.

Speaking of labels, professional interviewers do have a terminology of their own. Their professional jargon does not consist of a special vocabulary. In the United States – which is the only area which I have researched – personnel officers use the common English words that correspond to the concepts they want to convey but restrict them to exactly the meaning that is relevant to their purposes. They use these words as they are used in the training manuals for interviewers but nowhere is there any list of terms in such manuals nor does it appear that personnel managers are conscious of their specialized vocabulary. The fact is that all the employers which were interviewed for this project used a set of identical words in the same sense. They all knew what they were talking about but none had stopped to think about how they would verbalize the panoply of semantic features that each of these terms encompassed. All of the people I interviewed admitted that they had never stopped to really think about the matter. With regard to their specific concern about the meaning of the terms they used, they could be classified into three groups. The majority told me that they knew what they were talking about and so did their fellow personnel managers and there was no need to spend time on detailing the obvious. A small number of people bluntly told me that what I had in mind was strictly for academics and a downright waste of the precious time of people in their salary range as compared to professors whose time was less valuable. A few of my subjects were fascinated by the idea because it might help them to clarify their own knowledge of what they were doing. I particularly recall Mr. Michael C. Brandon, director of Corporate Communications at Northern Telecom Systems Corporation. Mr. Brandon had majored with honors in English some fifteen years ago and obviously had maintained an interest in language as an intellectual pursuit beyond his practical job of supervising the writing of P.R. releases and in-house publications. During our meeting he unwittingly manifested to me nonverbally what he liked in his applicants. When I started prodding in depth what he meant by certain terms and told him about the interest this had for my linguistic theory, he straightened his torso, leaned a bit forward, looked more intensely at me, while his pupils slightly dilated. He certainly was not in a hurry to finish the interview. He was keenly aware of all facets of verbal language and had some awareness of paralanguage but was rather surprised of how much importance he actually attributed to an applicant's nonverbal behavior. As he was evidently a low-kinesic person his surprise came as no surprise to me.

All interviewers pay attention to nonverbal behavior but not to the same degree and they certainly approach nonverbal perception from a different level of consciousness. One of my most fascinating meetings was with Mrs. Ida Cooney, vice-president for Corporate Communication of Hospital Corporation of America. Mrs. Cooney descends form a distinguished Italian family and although her native language is English as are her gestures, she is vivacious and high-kinesic. Mrs. Cooney appeared to be fully conscious of how she observes the nonverbal behavior of job applicants and we had such a good time talking about 'body language' that we almost forgot to talk about the impact of an applicant's verbal language and paralanguage. When describing a job candidate's verbal expressions this interviewer noted that she frankly disliked it when she was addressed as Ida rather than Mrs. Cooney. Being inappropriately addressed by one's first name is, of course, one of several instances where verbal language is perceived nonverbally. In this case, it is in the domain of proxemics, amounting to an invasion of one's private space. The inappropriate use of a first name or of a last name is the equivalent of coming too close or of remaining too distant. For Mrs. Cooney, who is in her fifties, being addressed by her first name by a young candidate was considered 'lack of respect' and I was reminded of the rules of dominance in deciding who determines the size of the inter-personal distance.

The terminology and the explanations for what it meant were identical across the sex and the race of the employers with whom I met during the three year research period.

Some interviewers take notes during the session, but most prefer to write down their impressions immediately after. The large companies tend to have standardized rating sheets. Such evaluation forms have rating scales for interpersonal skills, communication ability, motivation, attitude, stability, maturity, personality, and other factors that are to a large extent deduced from nonverbal manifestations. The only categories listed which overtly refer to body behavior are grooming, posture, manners, dress, and neatness.

Two such evaluation forms are shown on the next pages, one is for campus recruitment and the other is for the employment of experienced workers.

The College Interview Report, under the sub-heading of *Appearance*, lists five categories which are explicitly nonverbal: Grooming, posture, dress, manners, and neatness.

Some employment agency officers are also quite specific on matters of body physique. They do not like fat people. Fatness to them is synonymous with ill health, lack of energy, and even unwillingness to work hard. Business executives will only go so far as to express some reservations when an applicant is extraordinarily overweight. Even though fatness is not always a barrier, a 'lean look' is always an asset. Applicants have a feeling that obesity in women is more objectionable than in men.

One employer, from business, was kind enough to reveal his train of thought

Response?
Self-Reliant
Decision-Maker   Judgement

SINCERITY
Genuine Wholesome Attitude
Honest
Real

PERSONALITY
Enthusiasm   Total Individual
Industrious   Will Fit
Motivated   Likeable

QUALIFICATIONS
Academic Preparation
Work Experience
Fits Position Available

OVERALL EVALUATION
Long Range Potential
Drive and Ambition
Ability

PROBABLE ACTION

☐ OFFER   ☐ DELAY DECISION   ☐ WILL REFER TO _____

☐ INVITATION   ☐ NO INTEREST

CANDIDATE WILL BE CONTACTED?   ☐ YES   ☐ NO   BY WHAT DATE? _____

COLLEGE INTERVIEW REPORT

NAME _____   DATE OF _____
                                                    INTERVIEW

SCHOOL ADDRESS _____ PHONE _____ COLLEGE _____

HOME ADDRESS _____ DEGREE/MAJOR _____

CANDIDATE FOR _____ CUMULATIVE GRADE AVG. _____
                (Job Title)

PLEASE REPORT YOUR INTERVIEW IMPRESSIONS BY CHECKING THE MOST APPROPRIATE BOX

CHARACTERISTICS	Outstanding (A)	Above Average (B)	Satisfactory Acceptable (C)	Limited Potential (D)	Not Acceptable (E)
APPEARANCE					
Grooming					
Posture Manners					
Dress Neatness					
PREPARATION FOR INTERVIEW					
Knowledge of Company					
Knowledge of Positions Open					
Asked Pertinent & Relevant Questions					
EXPRESSION					
Organization Delivery					
Presentation					
Ideas					
DIRECTION					
Well Defined Goals					

SERVICE MERCHANDISE
(Catalog Showroom)

INTERVIEWER'S RATING SHEET

NAME OF APPLICANT _____

CANDIDATE FOR: _____ (Job Title)

DATE OF THIS INTERVIEW _____

INTERVIEWER: _____

PLEASE REPORT YOUR INTERVIEW IMPRESSIONS BY CHECKING THE MOST APPROPRIATE BOX IN EACH AREA

1. INTERPERSONAL SKILLS				
☐ NOT ASSERTIVE, ABRASIVE, ALOOF, WITHDRAWN, INTROVERTED.	☐ APPROACHABLE: SOMEWHAT RESERVED.	☐ WARM, SOCIABLE.	☐ VERY SOCIABLE AND OUTGOING.	☐ ASSERTIVE, EXTREMELY OUTGOING AND SOCIABLE— EXTROVERTED.
2. STABILITY				
☐ ILL AT EASE: IS "JUMPY" AND APPEARS NERVOUS.	☐ SOMEWHAT TENSE: IS EASILY IRRITATED.	☐ ABOUT AS POISED AS THE AVERAGE APPLICANT.	☐ CONFIDENT APPEARS TO TOLERATE PRESSURE MORE THAN AVERAGE PERSON.	☐ EXTREMELY WELL COMPOSED: APPARENTLY THRIVES UNDER PRESSURE.
3. MATURITY				
☐ IMMATURE NOT REALISTIC IN- FLEXIBLE.	☐ SOMEWHAT IMMATURE, IMPULSIVE.	☐ MATURE AND EVEN KEELED, ACTS APPROPRIATELY.	☐ MATURE GOOD PER- SPECTIVE FLEXIBLE, GOOD JUDGEMENT.	☐ EXTREMELY MATURE, FLEXIBLE YET DIS- PLAYS GOOD JUDGEMENT AND PERSPECTIVE.
4. COMMUNICATION ABILITY				
☐ TALKS VERY LITTLE EXPRESSES SELF POORLY	☐ TRIES TO EXPRESS SELF BUT DOES FAIR JOB AT BEST RAMBLES.	☐ AVERAGE FLUENCY AND EXPRESSION.	☐ TALKS WELL AND "TO THE POINT."	☐ EXCELLENT EXPRESSION: EXTREMELY FLUENT, FORCEFUL.
5. ALERTNESS				
☐ RATHER SLOW	☐ GRASPS IDEAS	☐ QUICK TO	☐ EXCEPTIONALLY KEEN AND ALERT

Category	☐	☐	☐	☐	☐
POOR KNOWLEDGE OF FIELD, NARROW SCOPED POOR RESULTS.	FAIR KNOWLEDGE OF FIELD AND RESULTS.	IS AS INFORMED AS THE AVERAGE APPLICANT, AVERAGE RESULTS.	FAIRLY WELL INFORMED; KNOWS MORE THAN AVERAGE APPLICANT, GOOD RESULTS.	HAS EXCELLENT KNOWLEDGE OF THE FIELD, BROAD GAUGED, OUTSTANDING RESULTS.	
7. EXPERIENCE	NO RELATIONSHIP BETWEEN APPLICANT'S BACKGROUND AND JOB REQUIREMENTS.	FAIR RELATIONSHIP BETWEEN APPLICANT'S BACKGROUND AND JOB REQUIREMENTS.	AVERAGE AMOUNT OF MEANINGFUL BACKGROUND AND EXPERIENCE.	BACKGROUND VERY GOOD CONSIDERABLE EXPERIENCE.	EXCELLENT BACKGROUND AND EXPERIENCE.
8. MOTIVATION	HAS POORLY DEFINED GOALS AND APPEARS TO ACT WITHOUT PLANNING AHEAD.	APPEARS TO SET GOALS TOO LOW AND TO PUT FORTH LITTLE EFFORT TO ACHIEVE THEM.	SETS GOALS APPROPRIATELY AND ACHIEVES THEM.	SETS GOALS HIGH AND WILLING TO GIVE EXTRA TO ACHIEVE.	SETS GOALS HIGH. SETS PLAN TO ACHIEVE GOALS.
9. ATTITUDE	NEGATIVE IN OUTLOOK TOWARD ASSOCIATES, SCHOOL AND WORK.	INDIFFERENT IN OUTLOOK TOWARD ASSOCIATES, SCHOOL AND WORK.	GOOD OUTLOOK TOWARD ASSOCIATES SCHOOL AND WORK.	VERY POSITIVE OUTLOOK TOWARD ASSOCIATES, SCHOOL AND WORK.	EXTREMELY POSITIVE OUTLOOK TOWARD ASSOCIATES, SCHOOL AND WORK.
10. EDUCATION	INAPPROPRIATE POOR SCHOLASTIC ACHIEVEMENT.	MEETS JOB REQUIREMENTS BUT PERFORMANCE OR SCHOOL QUALITY LESS THAN DESIRED.	APPROPRIATE SATISFACTORY GRADES.	VERY GOOD HIGH SCHOLASTIC ACHIEVEMENT.	EXTREMELY APPROPRIATE EXCELLENT SCHOLASTIC ACHIEVEMENT.
11. PROMOTABILITY	NOT PROMOTABLE.	FUTURE PROMOTABILITY SOMEWHAT LIMITED.	PROMOTABLE AFTER DEVELOPMENT.	GOOD POTENTIAL FOR FUTURE PROMOTIONS.	HIGH TALENT VERY PROMOTABLE NEEDS LITTLE DEVELOPMENT.
12. OVERALL	DEFINITELY UNSATISFACTORY.	SUBSTANDARD.	AVERAGE.	DEFINITELY ABOVE AVERAGE.	OUTSTANDING.

YOUR RECOMMENDATION (CHECK ONE):

☐ TURN DOWN

☐ BRING BACK FOR FURTHER INTERVIEWS

☐ EXTEND OFFER

☐ PLACE ON HOLD

INTERVIEW RATING SHEET (Continued)

LIST THE POSITIVE AND NEGATIVE ATTRIBUTES OF THE CANDIDATES BELOW.

PLUS

MINUS

after interviewing a heavy set man:

"The first thing I noticed was that he smiled and so he was not hostile but friendly. The second thing I noticed was his weight. And I immediately ran all kinds of things through my mind relating to past generalizations that have to do with someone who is this overweight. I started forming opinions about him before we even started talking based on the fact that he was overweight as much as he is; whether or not he could really get around, move around fast, in the fast pace that we keep in a rental store, in and out of the trucks and delivering merchandise and that sort of thing. I can't say that people are slow because they're overweight, it's just the preconceived notion that I have that a person may be slow because he is overweight."

When asked whether he would not hire this particular person because of his obesity, he replied: "Not just that alone. I would not necessarily not consider him for employment because he's overweight but because of the entire image that he presented, part of which was overweight." When asked about other aspects of this candidate, the employer said that he looked "good, neat and clean shaven" but that he "was very lacking in confidence", and that perhaps this impression related to his weight. When asked about what he considered the most negative feature of that candidate, he admitted that it was his weight and that 50% of the negative decision was due to the candidate's obesity.

There are strong government regulations protecting persons between the ages of 40 and 65. Employment counselors and job candidates, nevertheless, feel that evidence of the aging process in physical appearance has a negative effect and that this applies even more strongly for women than for men. It is illegal to ask an applicant for his age, his birthdate, or the ages of a woman's children or any other question that might seem designed to guess his age. An interviewer can legally ask whether the applicant can produce proof of age later on for insurance purposes. Persons between 40 and 65 years of age are a protected group and great care has to be taken to justify why they are not hired, and particularly in case they are dismissed. This means that the physical appearance of applicants who look fortyish is scrutinized with particular care while the potential employer makes his intelligent guesses. The applicant has the choice of either meeting the real or presumed prejudices against older people by acting young and enthusiastic, or of acting old and experienced so that he can have the advantages of fitting into a protected category.

Women are favored by the laws of affirmative action but to ask an applicant's sex is one of the many questions that the law forbids an interviewer to ask. I thought that it was a pretty irrelevant question anyway when one meets face-to-face with a candidate. Not so, I was told, in a period when companies try to fill their quota of female employees. Once an applicant showed up dressed like a woman but when this person came to the plant later on, she (or rather, he) arrived in men's clothing and this is what he biologically was.

Among the categories listed, the key characteristic is *neatness*. Interviewers say that the applicant's "image comes through his appearance". The *sine qua non* for an applicant to be considered for any job at all is that he be clean and neat. Crumpled or stained clothing, unkempt hair, or other signs of untidiness are totally unacceptable.

When the physical build, age and sex of persons viewed on videotape are highly similar, the rating of their differences in nonverbal behavior appears to be the same. Neither personality traits nor the halo effect seem to influence judgment. This was verified by showing two tapes of mock interviews to twenty undergraduate students at a two week interval in order to avoid a recency effect of the tape which had been viewed first. One tape depicted the same candidate in different nonverbal behaviors while the other tape showed six different candidates. Each tape consisted of six frames. The first five frames represented the same different types of nonverbal behavior in the same sequence while the sixth frame showed one type of nonverbal behavior on the first tape and a different one on the second tape. The usual rating sheet (see Appendix II) was administered on both occasions with the only difference that each student wrote his name on the sheet. A comparison of the answers for each student on his two sheets revealed that they were virtually the same with only three one-point variations in all for the identical nonverbal behaviors. The ratings for the sixth frame, on the contrary, were widely divergent.

Odor is probably the most intriguing body manifestation of all. In none of the personal meetings was it mentioned by the executives. When we brought it up to them, they looked somewhat embarrassed and said that they never thought of it, but many said that a bad body odor would automatically disqualify a candidate. As mentioned in the preceding chapter, the category 'odor', listed on the Hierarchy Survey questionnaire, received the highest ranking of objectionable features. During the personal meetings we spent some time discussing what was meant by unpleasant odor and found out that the worst type of odor is that of the unwashed. It is matched only by the alkaline odor of 'cheap soap'. Such unpleasant body odor is considered worse than stale breath.

A slight odor of sweat is permissible because that is unavoidable during the strain of an interview. Men should avoid too much after shaving lotion and women should go sparingly with their perfumes.

Grooming in the sixties referred very heavily to hair styles, but this is no longer a prime consideration as fashions have changed towards the more conservative look which business tends to favor anyway. Nobody objects to beards. Some men say that even though they personally dislike beards, this would not influence their judgment of a candidate. Some women like beards. Everybody insists that beards be well groomed and clean. Shaggy beards are unacceptable even for sociology professors. Women can have almost any hairdo as long as it is in style.

The *dress* code is defined as 'appropriate'. The latter is a key qualifier which comes up in regard to almost every type of artifact and behavior. Books on 'how to dress for success' abound. On the overall their advice is sound even though they do not mention enough that the dress code varies with the position for which the applicant is applying. It is in direct relation to the salary he is expecting. College seniors should come in suit and tie, but if everything else is fine, they may be invited for the second interview even if they wore casual clothing on the first interview as long as it was neat and not outrageous. On that second interview they are, however, expected to arrive in a well-cut suit and tie. The suit does not necessarily have to be the classic three-piece suit, but double knit polyester is definitely out. Men's legs are taboo. Socks should be long enough to cover the legs in the event the pants move up a bit while getting seated or changing positions. Socks that are crumpled or too short were mentioned by several employers. Although popular magazines frequently mention this fact (Soxology 1970) many college seniors which I questioned about this were not aware of it.

A women executive of a large national corporation told me that female applicants should always have a nice feminine touch about them in clothing and behavior lest they come across as overbearing. Men feel threatened by assertive women and women have to be infinitely more cautious than men in keeping the fine line between forcefulness and over-aggressiveness. Feminine attire is one of the ways a woman can soften the edge without compromising too heavily on showing that she does, indeed, possess the drive and motivation necessary for success in business.

Many executives remarked to me that if the job is not worth the effort to get dressed properly, the applicant obviously does not have enough interest in it to be considered. Others insisted that the candidate has to realize that one day he will represent the image of the company he wishes to join and that he has to understand that fact well enough to dress accordingly.

Interviewers spoke of 'appropriate' attire assuming that this was as clear a way of describing clothing as if they had said something like 'grey suit' or 'blue jacket'. Another qualifier that came up in connection with dress was 'polite'. When I asked what was meant by politeness I was told that an interviewee should show respect for the job he would like to perform, that his attire should indicate that he is serious about his plans for the future, that he should realize that if he joins the firm, his appearance will reflect on the company. Some interviewers told me to just look at them, they don't sit here in shirt sleeves while talking with me.

The latter remark reminds me of the similar-to-me effect which I will discuss extensively in the following chapter. One employment agency made a regular practice of sending a representative to the doors of companies at closing time and to lunch counters where certain employees would tend to gather. The manager of that employment agency carefully observed the clothing style of the employees in various companies. When she had applicants she would observe their attire and then try to send them to the firm whose employees dressed in a similar style. She had never heard of the similar-to-me effect but intuitively put it into practice, and quite successfully.

The category of *posture* frequently was associated with exactly the same qualifiers of appropriateness and politeness. While candidates mention 'correct' posture or that slumping is 'bad' posture, interviewers rarely speak in those descriptive terms. They seem to take these elementary facts for granted and concentrate on what in posture is indicative of an applicant's interest in the job and his attentiveness towards the interviewer. They look for forward leans as indices of excitement and enthusiasm, and sincere interest in the job for which he is being considered. They like candidates who shift posture when there is a change in argument or when the conversation touches highlights. They do not like quiet, static individuals.

My research supports the findings of research going on parallel at the time by McGovern and Ideus (1978) that the motionless candidate makes a very poor impression. Perfect composure is not at all stillness. It is forceful animation. Executives remarked that they do not want a nervous and certainly not an overbearing candidate, but that shifting one's posture or leg position shows alertness, confidence, self-respect, and energy. The latter is the vital ingredient everybody is looking for. Most executives want a 'slightly aggressive' candidate.

In a videotape that was rated by 28 personnel managers I showed the same young white male candidate saying the same things. In one frame he was animated and what one could call moderately aggressive, and in the other frame he leaned forward on the table to the limits of his territoriality. The two frames were not shown consecutively but within a sequence of other video frames so

Rating of Rrame III (strongly aggressive)
and Frame V (moderately aggressive)
by professional personnel managers.

Males (=21, age range 24-26)		Females (N=7, age 24-57)	
III	V	III	V

1. a) Would you hire the applicant? Yes No b) If yes, would you hire the applicant: a) enthusiastically b) without reservations c) with reservations

16 yes, 5 no	16 yes, 5 no	6 yes, 1 no	5 yes, 2 no
2a 8b 6c	2a 8b 6c	5b 1c	2b 3c

2. The applicant's intellectual capacity is: a) outstanding b) average c) below average

9a 11b 1c	7a 13b 1c	3a 3b 1c	6b 1c

3. The applicant appears: a) self-reliant b) insecure c) overbearing

17a 2b 2c	16a 1b 4c	6a 1c	6b 1c

4. Does the applicant appear emotionally stable? Yes No

18 yes, 3 no	18 yes, 3 no	6 yes, 1 no	6 yes, 1 no

5. Does the applicant appear: a) highly competent b) adequately competent c) incompetent

6a 14b 1c	7a 13b 1c	3a 3b 1c	6b 1c

6. Outside of any professional consideration I would like to have the applicant as: a) a personal friend b) as an acquaintance c) as my boss d) as my employee e) never have anything to do with him.

3a 3b 12d	3a 4b 1c	1b 1c 5d	1c 5d 1e
3e	8d 5e		

as not to make apparent the type of comparison I had in mind. The rating forms were the same ones that I used throughout this research project. (See Appendix I and II) The 21 male interviewers hardly distinguished between the two while the 7 female interviewers favored the more strongly aggressive candidate to be hired without reservations. They also found him slightly more competent than the only moderately aggressive candidate. On the preceding page is the compilation of the replies from the rating sheets.

One interviewer told me that a 'stiff' candidate made him suspicious. "What is he holding back?" Some executives feel that they have to try to help the candidate to 'feel more at ease' before they give up on him.

To solicit changes in posture some executives will change their own seating arrangement during the session from a vis-a-vis position behind a table or desk to the side-by-side position next to the applicant; or they will invite the applicant to join him over to the club chair and coffee table corner of the room. While this goes on, they carefully observe postural movements of the applicant and his ambulation when there is a change of chairs. The general body behavior expected of a successful candidate is one of self-control coupled with forceful aggressiveness.

Above all, interviewers look for 'rapport'. When I asked how they figure out that an applicant has established rapport with them, at first I got the usual answer that they "just know it", "feel it", are "experienced in knowing it", "get the right vibes". It usually takes me a little while to prod what external manifestation causes such feelings. Eventually, interviewers agree that they see posture sharing between the candidate and themselves. They also deduce rapport from the direction of an applicant's posturing towards the interviewer and from the ease with which he moves his body, in slow continuous movements rather than in abrupt movements that "give an impression of insincerity". Nervous movements are expected from young candidates especially at the beginning of the interview but should subside with time.

Fidgeting is universally interpreted as a sign of nervousness. But, unless fidgeting is very distracting and continuous there is great variation on its evaluation. Some interviewers feel that fidgeting shows lack of maturity while others are fairly forgiving considering the tension and pressure of the interview situation. A certain amount of fidgeting is taken for granted in college seniors and to a lesser degree in applicants from business school without working experience. It is tolerated only in a minimal form and duration in applicants for jobs beyond the entry level. Older men are more lenient towards fidgeting and women are extremely irritated by it. If everything else is very good, a fidgeting candidate will be invited for a second interview, but on that occasion he should not exhibit fidgeting behavior. Fidgeting, in particular, is judged in relation to the prospective job. It fully excludes someone from becoming an insurance saleman, but a moderate amount of it may be tolerated in an accountant in the back office.

The category of *manners* encompasses all the above. Posture is a large part of it. In my conversations with interviewers, the word manners was never volunteered. Several persons spoke of 'breeding', of 'projecting the proper behavior'. Some mention was made about candidates 'walking in a polite manner', of waiting to be offered a seat rather than just grabbing a chair, of not interrupting, of getting up when a lady or an older man entered the room.

6.3. *Proxemics*

Mention of *personal space* was never brought up spontaneously by any of the employers whom we contacted during our personal meetings. When I brought up this topic, the consensus was that applicants really make mistakes in this area. From my observations of ongoing interview sessions I can only tell that a slightly larger distance is kept when the parties are not of the same sex. The majority of interviews take place across a coffee table, and one interviewer told me that candidates feel more at ease when he sits next to them in the side-by-side position.

Most categories of evaluation on standard forms do not overtly refer to nonverbal behavior but in reality nonverbal behavior is an extensive component of them. Some categories, such as interpersonal skills, motivation, attitude, stability, maturity, and personality rely almost exclusively on the applicant's nonverbal behavior for how he is rated.

Most executives will say that the most important area of evaluation is *oral communication*. When asked to specify what they mean by this, it becomes clear that the term covers the candidate's skill of communication which includes clarity and conciseness of verbal expression conjoined with directness of posture, eye contact, a moderate amount of appropriate gesticulation, slight postural shifts to signal emphasis or a change of topic, and an alert facial expression. All these aspects were said to be relevant indicators when the topic of communicative skills came up in the personal meetings. Some of these aspects were directly mentioned by the executives and all of the remaining were immediately recognized when I mentioned them as possible criteria for the evaluation of communication ability.

Impediments to 'good oral communication' were considered to be vague, lengthy answers, empty pauses and hesitation words, unclear enunciation, and the nonverbal factors of lack of directness in posture, avoidance of eye contact, fidgeting, and excessive stillness of body motion. It is also of the utmost importance that the candidate demonstrate good listening behavior through an attentive posture. None of the people who listed all these body motions under the heading of 'oral communication' were the least disturbed by the fact that most of what they attributed to effective oral communication was not 'oral' at all. As I said before, personnel officials use common vocabulary in a specialized sense. Oral communication means communication *tout court* and that implies effective communication which, of course, includes language, paralanguage, and kinesics. The qualifier 'oral' is not in contrast to non-oral but inclusive of it. This derives from the obsolete idea that the only function of nonverbal behavior is to underline verbalization. Good oral communication is supposed to be supported by non-oral means. The fact remains that judgment was primarily based on those supporting elements. The secondary features in reality were primary.

The next item that was most frequently volunteered by the executives which I interviewed was *eye contact*. Mutual gaze is the nonverbal behavior of which interviewers are keenly aware. It is mentioned not only in connection with certain impressions but is overtly mentioned as a manifestation which is purposely observed and openly discussed qua manifestation. Next to neatness eye contact is the *sine qua non* for job consideration. In the hierarchy of importance eye contact with the interviewer ranks highest. Good eye contact indicates honesty, confidence (also called 'self-pride'), and determination. A 'shine in the eye' shows alertness and interest.

Lack of eye contact is the one behavior which will adversely affect even an otherwise best qualified applicant. Failure to maintain eye contact indicates shyness, insecurity, nervousness, lack of general motivation and drive, lack of interest in the particular job for which the candidate is being considered, and may even indicate untruthfulness. All executives said that any candidate who fails to maintain eye contact during most of the interview session will not be invited back. The results from my videotape tests showed that an applicant may well reveal that he comes perfectly prepared for the interview when he says, "I've done a great deal of research in our library, and I've reviewed the *Standard and Poor's* and the *Moody's* indexes . . ." but will cancel any good impression when he does not look at the interviewer. He may inform the interviewer that in the past he has been "working with corporate officials of major organizations", but the message gets lost when he stares at the ceiling. Interviewers know that good eye contact does not mean staring the other in the eye, but it is the normal exchange process of the on and off contact of mutual gaze (Argyle and Cook

1976). This is what they are looking for.

Hiring officials speak of the need for 'energetic' employees. A natively high level of *energy* is required of all candidates but the level of 'forcefulness' a candidate is expected to show depends on the type of job for which he is being considered. This distinction was explained to be by Mr. Bud Curtis, an executive with a large insurance company. People destined for sales related work may even be a bit too aggressive for the normal, conservative taste of interviewers. The best candidate for any type of work should combine courtesy and self-control ('manners') with 'drive'. Judgement of an applicant's degree of 'drive and energy' is formed from observing his body motions. Signs of 'forcefulness' I have already mentioned earlier in connection with postural behavior and eye contact.

Interviewers like for the candidate to 'punctuate' what he says with *hand gesticulation.* By this they mean the use of illustrators (movements that are intimately tied to the content and/or flow of speech). Among those they look primarily for batons (movements which emphasize a phrase, clause, sentence, or group of sentences). Employers tolerate but do not appreciate the other types of Ekman's illustrators (Ekman 1980: 98). Emblems were never mentioned and self-manipulators, at best, are excused in the beginner. The latter were classified under fidgeting.

Wild and excessive gesticulating is considered very negatively and as a sign of an overbearing personality or as a symptom of more uncontrolled nervousness than fidgeting. 'Proper' gesticulation is evaluated in relation to what is said and in relation to what it implies about the candidate. Appropriate gesticulation is very positive. It shows clarity of expression and is indicative of a forceful and enthusiastic personality.

A candidate who does not gesticulate at all while talking is believed to lack drive and motivation. As said before, all employers want an energetic individual. Stillness is equated with dullness.

How much better a candidate comes across when he 'properly punctuates' what he says was apparent when I counted the illustrators of a successful candidate compared to those of an unsuccessful one. I was lucky to have a student, Tyler H. Harrison, who got interested in my interview research. He contacted another student, Gina C. McNeal, whose father owns a supply house for the rental of domestic appliances in Marietta, Georgia. The two convinced Mr. Perry J. McNeal, president of McNeal Management Incorporated, to videotape two live interviews. Even more luck was on my side when one of these two interviewees was hired and the other was not. These interviews were chosen for no other reason but that they took place during the Thanksgiving recess when the two students were able to leave the university and go to Marietta, Georgia. The opening for which the job candidates applied was that of manager-trainee in Network Rental, the trade name of NcNeal Management. Each interview lasted about the same amount of time; the successful one 30 minutes and 45 seconds, and the unsuccessful one 27 minutes. Both candidates were white males in their mid-twenties.

The successful applicant had a total of 121 illustrators which amounts to a total of 4.48 gesticulations per minute. Of these, 40 were single-hand gestures, amounting to a total of 1.48 per minute; 81 were double-hand gestures amounting to a total of 3 per minute.

The unsuccessful applicant had a total of 55 illustrators, which amounts to a total of 0.96 gesticulations per minute. Of these, 46 were single-hand gestures, amounting to a total of 0.67 per minute; 9 were double-hand gestures amounting to a total of 0.29 per minute.

Of course, there was more to the difference between the two interviewees than hand gesticulations. In looking at the video tapes this was, however, what impressed me as the most salient distinction between the parties. Mr. McNeal himself gave as the major reason for not hiring the kinesically quiet candidate that he did not show enthusiasm and not even a great deal of interest in the job for which he was applying.

"The only moment he started moving on his chair and gesticulating was when he spoke about a memorable experience of his own. The rest of the time he did not move around in his chair and seemed so monotonous that he almost put me to sleep."

Mr. McNeal also remarked that "the more enthusiastic a person is the more gestures he tends to have". Although he had his share of abrasive interviewees he "cannot remember any instance when I [he] thought someone was gesturing too much".

6.4. Conclusion

The perfect applicant is forceful and eager, self-controlled and well-mannered, arrives well-prepared for the interview and expresses himself with clarity and concision.

The results of my research have been summarized on the following little handout called 'Tips for Interviewing'. Some job applicants have already made use of these suggestions and told me that they found them to be helpful hints. A follow-up research project is planned on the success rate of candidates using the practical application that emerged from this type of research.

— TIPS FOR INTERVIEWING —

Walburga von Raffler-Engel
Vanderbilt University

BE NEAT

(a) Emphasize your personal hygiene but make certain you do not smell of soap, after shaving lotion, or perfume.

(b) Dress conservatively: Women should wear an attractive but not provocative dress or a suit (no pantsuits) and men should wear a well-cut suit with tie.

BE FORCEFUL AND EAGER

(c) Keep eye contact with your interviewer. Neither slouch on your chair nor sit still like a mummy. Occasionally, you may bend forward slightly.

(d) Try not to fidget nervously but be animated using appropriate hand gestures and have a lively facial expression.

BE WELL PREPARED AND COMMUNICATE CLEARLY

(e) Research the company for which you are interviewing and the job for which you are applying.

(f) Formulate your answers concisely and express them with clarity and good enunciation. Do not talk about experiences that are not relevant to the job.

Our research indicates that your first impression is extremely important. Concentrate on the interview as soon as you walk in the room. We also found that women interviewers tend to be more critical than men interviewers and that both get more severe as they grow older.

7. THE SIMILAR-TO-ME EFFECT

As I mentioned before, the director of one employment agency regularly observes the attire of the managers coming out of the major local firms at lunch time and sees to it that the prospective employees that are sent to those firms happen to match the style of clothing that is prevalent in that particular place. Employment specialists seem to do this instinctively, unaware of the fact that there is a certain amount of psychological research on the "similar to me effect". (Evans 1963; Golightly *et al.* 1972; Nahemow and Lawton 1975; Rand and Wexley 1975, 1976; Wexley *et al.* 1977).

It is natural for people to search out people that are similar to them and feel more congenial and more relaxed in their company than with people that have dissimilar outlooks on life, working habits, social concerns, and intellectual pursuits. People tend to cluster within their race, their ethnic background, their age range, their sex, level of education and social status, and within their professional group.

People also tend to like those whom they perceive as being similar to themselves, at least in the initial stages of meeting such people. It does not mean that people cannot form close friendships across races and ages or social conditions but it requires more effort to get to know and appreciate people that are dissimilar from ourselves and not everybody is willing to make the effort. According to the research on the job interview by Rand and Wexley (1975), the similar-to-me effect plays a significant role in the evaluation of an applicant as interviewers tend to give a better rating to candidates who have characteristics similar to their own.

Psychologists believe that the 'similar-to-me effect' operates below consciousness. I believe that in many instances it is quite conscious albeit not admittedly, and that sometimes interviewers are fully aware that they judge from the vantage point of themselves as a model. This idea came to me when I heard several of the executives with whom I met saying that an applicant's college grade point average is of little importance except for technical jobs, such as engineering. For office jobs or a career in sales, a list of extra-curricular activities might be a better indicator of his potential. Sometimes an executive would then smile telling me that he has an excellent salary plus option on shares and in college he had a C average. Others, on the contrary, would tell me that good grades are indicative of intelligence and that this is always an asset. As many of the employers with whom I met were alumni of the university where I teach, I had easy access to their academic record. True enough, the importance an employer attributed to a job applicant's grade point average was in direct relation to his own scholastic record.

I already mentioned that high-kinesic interviewers are more conscious of an applicant's gesticulations than low-kinesic individuals. I also discovered that the observations interviewers made about clothing could be easily matched against their own attire. An executive woman mentioned that she likes candidates to dress with some imagination and not to look like they were wearing a uniform. This lady was dressed in the classic business suit but with several very attractive personal touches. It was clear that she liked in others what she liked for herself.

Where interviewers are most conscious of wanting a person with tastes and characteristics similar to themselves is when they analyze an applicant's behavior for his capacity for getting along with people. Even if they do not expect to work closely with the applicant should he join the firm, they unconsciously assume that if he can get along with them, he can get along with others. To form their judgment in this respect, they look for 'rapport'. As said above, the behavior which they perceive of as indicative of 'rapport' is postural synchrony – which is a movement similar to one of their own. Rand and Wexley (1975) found that the more a candidate was perceived as similar to the interviewer, the more suitable, more knowledgeable, and more competent he was judged to be. I am tempted to conclude that the tendency of white Anglo-Saxon males to hire males of similar background, and possibly also graduates of their own alma mater may not be a form of racism, chauvinism, and provincialism – albeit this may sometimes be the case – as much as an instinctual consequence of the similar-to-me effect.

In conclusion, if one has confidence in oneself it is natural to look in others for equally superior characteristics. Secondly, if one has to work in a congenial atmosphere, the easiest way to achieve this is within a homogenious group. It takes great maturity and, above all, patience to adjust to the behavior of people who are very different from ourselves. In the following chapter, I mention the difficulty men have in deciding whether or not to shake hands with women applicants. The similar-to-me effect may be the greatest barrier to minorities when they apply for jobs. It does not represent an inherent prejudice against anybody. It is really an unconscious preference of self over others. In its mild form it is a normal part of the human psyche. In its extreme form it is the basis of conceitedness and of prejudice.

Popular magazines and books constantly advise those who want to "climb the corporate ladder" to "conform in dress and manners". This is sound advice when it is done with tastefulness and restraint. Employers are aware of the attempt of job seekers to conform and when I discussed the meaning of 'rapport' some interviewers warned me that posture mirroring can be overdone. They told me that they watch out for artificial conformity and that they carefully distinguish it from spontaneous interactional synchrony.

Sales people are well aware of the importance of coming across as similar to their prospective customer (Weisberg and von Raffler-Engel 1980; Moine 1982) but some customers are quite alert to such persuasion techniques. The similar-to-me effect is not just a simple outward phenomenon. It affects complex covert similarities. An executive may like loud ties for himself but prefer his junior managers to have more conservative tastes. To 'be in sync' with such an executive, one should sense that distinction which he makes and not simplistically conform to that one aspect of his choice in clothing. Most interviewees know the rules of the dominance relationship but are not aware of them in all their nuances. In a similar vein, if an interviewer smokes, he may not necessarily appreciate that same vice in a candidate. When the executives that I met mentioned that they go by 'a feeling' they may have put what they do in the most scientific terms possible, at least until we have a more precise knowledge and descriptive power to classify all the fine shades involved in interactional behavior.

The similar-to-me effect equally affects the candidate. He may intuitively like or dislike the man who interviews him, and the latter will sense this. An interviewer will also sense attempts at faking such liking. It is more difficult to detect unsincere expressions in persons with whose life habits one is not familiar than in persons whose background one shares. Interviewers do not only want to associate harmoniously with their employees, they also want to be certain that they understand them and are not misled by them. Many of the consequences of the similar-to-me effect, consciously and/or unconsciously as it may be perceived, influence the interview. I will discuss it more at length in the chapter on minority hiring. Controversial results in research on likeness among interactants can probably be solved if one takes into account that as much as we tend to like people that are similar to us in many aspects, we do not necessarily look for a mirror image of ourselves in all situations, especially when we look for somebody to perform a task for us which is not identical to what we ourselves do. This might explain the inconclusive results on likeness in matching salesmen and customers in the research by Evans (1963). Other findings which are inconclusive because of inadequate research designs are reported by Hulbert and Capon (1972: 29).

The similar-to-me effect is pervasive but research in this area is still in its beginning. I will come back to it in the chapter on minority interviewing.

8. THE STRUCTURE OF THE CAREER INTERVIEW

8.1. *The structure of the interview*

As said before, like all speech acts the interview is divided into three parts: speech preparatory, speech central, and speech final (Jones and von Raffler-Engel 1981).

In the particulars of the career interview the speech preparatory section begins immediately when the two conversation partners see each other. If verbally the speech act begins with the spoken greeting formula, the face-to-face interaction begins even before the nonverbal initiation of the greeting formula, the slight smile, and head tilt. It begins when people decide whether or not they want to acknowledge each other. In the context of the job interview it begins when the interviewer sees the candidate, whether or not the candidate has already visualized him in the room. The interviewer starts sizing up the applicant as soon as he enters the room. He observes how the applicant closes the door and how he advances in the room before the interviewer initiates the conversation with the greeting formula. Some interviewers hesitate a moment before offering a chair to the candidate because they want to observe his reaction. It is considered highly improper if an applicant starts selecting a chair of his own choosing even if he does not sit down until the interviewer invites him to do so. It is the interviewer who points towards the sofa or chair where he wants the candidate to seat himself. The executive of a large national corporation with whom I met told me that whenever a candidate picks out a chair other than the one he had in mind he finds this very irritating. There are many subtle motions which the candidate is supposed to pick up. It begins with the degree of formality of the setting.

In many cases, the applicant has been pre-screened by the receptionist or secretary who brings in the dossier before the candidate enters the room. In some offices she is encouraged in passing to make a brief comment about the candidate, in others she is supposed only to quietly bring in the material but employers admit that they can tell from her facial expression what she thinks about the candidate.

Employers admittedly pay a great deal of attention to 'the first impression'. They do so particularly when recruiting on college campuses and business schools and to a somewhat lesser extent when hiring experienced people. A small number of interviewers state that they do not pay great attention to the first minute or two of the interview because they feel that this so largely depends on how they themselves structure it. All interviewers admit that they get some impression of the candidate as soon as they see him, but not all consider this an integral part of their conscious evaluation. When asked how often their first impression coincided with their final evaluation, of 35 interviewers which I surveyed, 26 said that they seldom changed their mind after the first two minutes had passed.

Given that the job interview is a process of evaluation of the personality of the candidate more than an exchange of information, it might appear arbitrary to divide the encounter into any parts. There is, nevertheless, a strong rationale for keeping the traditional subdivisions. The content of the speech central part varies distinctly from that of the preparatory and final parts. Nonverbally the speech central section allows for kinesic synchrony, posture shifts to accompany shifts in topic of conversation, and most of all for speech accompanying and speech substituting gesticulation, for the synchronization of speech tempo, and for chronemics, the timing of the interval between question and answer. The gamut of nonverbal activities in the peripheral sections is restricted in both time and scope. Unfortunately my data do not include information on how heavy the central section weighs in the overall evaluation of the candidate compared to the other sections.

Least is known on the importance of the speech final section albeit considerable information is available on the leave-taking ritual. The end of the interview is firmly signalled to the applicant when the employer stands up. Sometimes he will accompany the applicant to the door and sometimes not. This nonverbal manifestation is dependent on the desire or not to see more of the candidate, who may or may not be invited for the second interview. One employer, Mr. McNeal (see preceding chapter) feels that when he has interviewed an excellent candidate, at this stage there is a role reversal. It is the employer who wants to make certain that the candidate accepts a forthcoming offer. This is signified to the candidate by the full accompanying walk to the door and maybe a bit beyond.

Many interviewers mention the *handshake.* They show an intense dislike for the 'fishy' handshake, are forgiving of nervous sweaty palms, and like a 'hearty' squeeze. Such a 'firm, manly handshake' is said to be indicative of confidence. With women male interviewers don't yet quite know much about what to do and whether to shake hands at all. Most feel relieved when the woman does not extend her hand but if handshake they must, they refrain from

THE STRUCTURE OF THE CAREER INTERVIEW 67

any judgment because admittedly they do not know how to interpret a woman's handshake.

In the literature the 'fishy' handshake is the one most frequently mentioned. Mortimer Feinberg, president of Bonney-Fessenden Sociograph Associates and professor of psychology at Baruch College of the City University of New York, in a handout on *Getting personal: Sabotage by body language*, sent to me by my former student Keith Newman, writes the following:

"An analysis of the fish handshaker goes like this: He is ill at ease, he isn't used to shaking hands and he probably detests being touched. He may or may not have been politely brought up, but he has a strong inclination to feel superior to the person with whom he is forced to shake hands. He's probably arrogant – most arrogant people shy away from human contact because they never know through which physical gesture their arrogance will seep."

In discourse analysis three functions are generally distinguished: the referential, the regulatory, and the affective (von Raffler-Engel 1980a). The personality of an individual comes across through all three functions when he speaks as well as when he listens. Even in the interview situation it is nevertheless useful to keep the three functions distinct at least in the first stages of the analysis.

The referential, or informative, function is largely restricted to the speech central section of the interview. In the interview situation nonverbal behavior accompanying informative statements is judged in two different manners. In its normative function it is judged as part of the communicative prowess of the candidate. He is expected to express himself clearly and concisely and his gesticulation is evaluated inasmuch as it helps or hinders the communication of his message. In addition, it also becomes a means for judging the energy level of the applicant.

The regulatory or interactional function covers the largest portion of the two peripheral sections. The answer to the question of how the candidate can get along with people is very much evaluated on how well he handles the flow of the conversation, on how well he perceives the paralinguistic and nonverbal cues to take the speaker turn or to relinquish it. It is probably the most important function during this particular type of face-to-face interaction.

The affective, or emotive, function is present throughout the interview. The latter is of extreme interest and monitored by the parties involved almost in a cat-and-mouse game fashion. Both parties admittedly try to hide their ego-state. In the barter of any business transaction nobody will give away all his cards. With particular regard to the interview situation, control over cues to one's ego-state is paramount. The interviewee does not want to show his nervousness or lower his bargaining power by being overly eager. In some instances the interviewer even more than the interviewee will be compelled to hide his true feelings.

8.2. Dominance

This brings us to the inter-personal relationship that obtains in the dyad. It may involve a dominant partner and a conversation partner that is in the subordinate role throughout the interaction. Or, it may involve a peer relationship where dominance and subordination waver in a constantly changing pattern. In most instances the interviewer is clearly the dominant partner except, as said before, when he is trying to hire a very important candidate. In any case, and particularly with a candidate who has to be rejected, the interviewer has to keep in mind that he always is both buyer and seller. He represents his company and has to leave a positive image behind. Any outward show of negative emotions has to be checked. The fact that an interviewer represents the image of his company has to be constantly kept in mind was mentioned in several of the meetings with executives.

Interviewers are well aware of the dominance pattern. Some of the training booklets advise that the interviewer should make certain that "he guides the interview from opening to closing to insure that the applicant never gains control of the session" (in-house Handbook on Interviewing Skills of Service Merchandise, courtesy of Mr. Kenneth Brewer). One executive told me that if an interviewee tries to take over during the session this automatically disqualifies him.

8.3. Psychological tests

If an interviewer observes something weird in an otherwise desirable candidate, he cannot legally probe very deep. He may, however, request that potential employees undergo psychological testing. Such tests and the use of the polygraph must be administered by trained professionals. Certified psychologists may ask anything they want to ask including questions about the use of drugs, past and present. The literature on psychological testing is exhaustive and, thus, there is no need for me to go into it. The polygraph is very interesting to students of nonverbal behavior. It picks up a body motion that cannot be noticed by the naked eye. Experienced interviewers, however, say that they have become almost as sensitive as the machine. Not that they can perceive the tiny amount of sweat which only the polygraph can pick up, but they detect enough minute concomitant bodily manifestations that they are able to sum up. Candidates generally control hand tremor, but are seldom aware of a slight quiver in the voice, a minuscule change in breathing, muscle tensing, movements of the eye lids, and manifestations of stress release when the interviewer abandons the difficult terrain and goes on to another question.

8.4. Conclusion

In essence, what interviewers do is try to detect competence from performance. They observe their candidates for indices of the desired competency as they cannot directly test the latter. Firestone (1982: 10) provides the clearest description of this process with an example:

"When a customer enters a store looking for a salesperson, there is no sure way to recognize which salesperson is most competent until some behavior has been communicated. Performance of these behaviors is not competency, but rather gives evidence from which it may be inferred that the competency is present."

9. THE RELATIONSHIP OF NONVERBAL FEATURES
TO VERBAL FEATURES IN THE EVALUATION PROCESS

What potential employers have in mind when they interview is to find the most competent and cooperative person for the job among all the candidates that have applied for that opening. The research project reported in this book has attempted to identify the nonverbal cues which lead to the decision for hiring or rejecting an applicant. It is obvious that verbal cues also play a large role in the selection process but their examination is not within the confines of this project. I felt that there was not much need for such a research because the subject is amply covered in the literature. What has been missing all along was a comprehensive study on the nonverbal component and a study of how the nonverbal component interacts with the verbal one. The first research to determine how much weight nonverbal behavior had when measured against verbal behavior was conducted in 1978 and presented at the Second Congress of the International Association for Semiotic Studies in Vienna in 1979 (von Raffler-Engel *et al.* 1980).

The idea for this research had its origin in what to the student of nonverbal behavior was a puzzling experience. I showed to my class in Nonverbal Communication at Vanderbilt University a videotape which had been prepared by the Owen Graduate School of Management of that same university for the training of business school graduates for a successful career interview. This videotape consisted of two sections, one depicting the perfect interviewee and the other one showing the most common mistakes an interviewee can make. The two men who are seen on the screen are Prof. William Dickson of the Owen School of Management and Mr. Andrew Spohn, then Personnel Director of Genesco, Inc. in Nashville, Tennessee and now a Vice-President of the Chase Manhattan Bank in New York City. They have taken turns so that each appears once as interviewer and once as interviewee. The perfect interviewee is impersonated by Mr. Spohn and the bumbling applicant is portrayed by Prof. Dickson.

The good applicant answers questions head-on and is specific about his capacities and career goals. He is knowledgeable about the firm to which he is applying, having consulted the appropriate research sources such as Standard and Poor's Register of Corporations, Directors and Executives. He sits erect, keeps eye contact with the interviewer, and maintains the same face-to-face distance throughout the interview. He gesticulates at frequent intervals using small range, incisive, nonrepetitive illustrators, makes a very limited use of emblems, and is virtually free of adaptors.

The poor applicant gives rambling answers, defines his capabilities with only vague statements like 'working with people', and is unspecific about his career goals. He has not done his homework on the opening for which he applies. He sometimes looks down or gazes in the air and covers his mouth with his hand when speaking. He frequently slouches on his chair; when he establishes eye contact he leans forward across the table that separates him from the interviewer and invades the latter's personal space. He uses few, but wide range illustrators and makes almost constant use of self- and object-adaptors.

Both the poor and the good applicant are dressed in a well-cut tailored suit and tie. After viewing the tape, I spoke with Prof. Dickson asking him to summarize for me what he did when impersonating the poor applicant, and he replied that he tried to make all the mistakes he had encountered from inexperienced job applicants with his evasive, broad statements. When I asked Prof. Dickson whether he had also tried to show inadequate postural behavior, he said that no, he had not thought of this. Prof. Dickson was astonished when told that he looked as unimpressive nonverbally as he sounded verbally. Obviously, unconsciously, he had either mimicked some unsuccessful applicant or, more likely, given the natural co-occurrence between verbal and nonverbal behavior, 'sloppy' verbal behavior is automatically accompanied by 'sloppy' nonverbal behavior. Even Prof. Dickson's tie had slightly gone off-center. An experienced teacher and public speaker, Prof. Dickson was not likely to be nervous, but in his personification of an unacceptable candidate, he fidgeted slightly and exhibited a considerable amount of self-adaptors.

At the end of the interview sessions, Mr. Spohn is shown alone explaining that hiring companies no longer give extensive tests to prospective employees and rely instead on individual interviews. He then goes on advising job applicants on how to conduct themselves during the interview. He explains that organizations seek information on the applicant's past experience, his accomplishments, his career goals, and his behavior during the interview. With particular respect to the latter, Mr. Spohn does not mention nonverbal behavior except for the following counsel: "Dress neatly; have a good hair cut; present a good image. The first impression has lasting effect."

We all commented on the fact that the poor applicant has disqualified himself as much by his nonverbal behavior as he had done by his inappropriate verbalizations. The class discussed at length whether irritating behavior would automatically disqualify an otherwise adequate interviewee. Consequently, we engaged in a series of research projects to study the relationship of verbal and nonverbal behavior in the perception of the job applicant by professional, semi-professional and nonprofessional judges. I contacted Mr. Spohn and Prof. Dickson, who were most cooperative and gave permission for the use of the tape in any form suitable for my research.

Then with the assistance of Keith Newman, one of my students who had a good grasp of handling technical equipment and the necessary patience to cope with the tedious job of selective dubbing, I altered the original Dickson-Spohn tape to serve as an instrument to test the relationship of verbal and nonverbal elements in the judgment of this particular type of communicative interaction.

9.1. *Research design*

To eliminate the personality factor in judging different applicants, I decided to superimpose the voice of the good applicant to the body of the poor applicant and vice versa. To produce such an instrument, the Dickson-Spohn video-tape was divided into ten small segments of an average duration of 50 seconds each. The segments were selected primarily on the basis of their feasibility for dubbing. This, unfortunately, left out some of the kinesically most offensive behaviors, like when the poor applicant jiggled his coffee cup in a manner which had produced a feeling of nervousness among my students when they had been viewing the original tape. On the other hand, the advantage of the division into segments was that in each segment a specific nonverbal behavior can be matched against the rating and it is thus possible to assess the impact of particular movements and the degree of offensiveness depending on range, velocity, duration and orientation of otherwise identical movements.

Parenthetically, what strikes one when comparing the short segments with the original long videotape is the fact that a fidgeting movement is felt as irritating only when it is protracted over time. A brief adaptor causes little, if any, irritation in the viewer. What needs further research is to find out how a live face-to-face reaction may differ from reacting to a moving picture.

9.2. *Instrument*

The experimental instrument eventually consisted of a videotape divided into two parts, each of which consisted of five segments. The first part showed the poor behavior and the good verbal content and the second part showed the good body behavior and the poor verbal content. An interval of one minute was left blank after each segment. During that interval a Roman numeral appeared on the screen corresponding to an identical numeral on the rating sheet and which represented the previously viewed segment in sequential order.

9.3. Testing procedure

To allow for possible weaknesses in the dubbing the raters were apologetically told by the technician operating the camera that his videotape was not of first quality. The experimenter then explained the testing procedures to the subjects.

All five video frames were shown to be raters in their numbered sequence and during a single session. After viewing each frame the raters had one minute to compile an identical forced-choice rating sheet consisting of six multiple-choice questions. At the end of the entire tape the subjects were asked to give a short overall evaluation of the applicant. (See Rating Sheet in Appendix.)

An identical videotape was subsequently prepared inverting the sequence of presentation, thus showing the good body behavior and the poor verbal content first. (Whether the sequence of presentation has any bearing on the evaluation will be determined by subsequent analogous testing procedures sometime in the future.) After the dubbed tape had been readied, an additional tape was prepared with the identical segments from the original tape to function as control.

9.4. Subjects

The two contrasting dubbed tapes were evaluated by raters of compatible background. All the judges were employees of the Vanderbilt University Personnel Office. Not all had actually interviewed job applicants, but all were familiar with job applicant evaluation procedures. The subjects were randomly selected by Dr. Henrietta Davis, Chief of Personnel at Vanderbilt University at that time. After eliminating all answer sheets which had only sporadic answers and thus had to be disqualified, the number of judges was fourteen, seven for each of the two videotapes. The first group consisted of seven female raters and the second group had six females and one male.

After I had tested the two groups of personnel office employees, I showed the two dubbed tapes to twenty-seven (27) undergraduate students at Vanderbilt University, none of whom had ever taken a course with me. Of the test results, three had to be disqualified because they had completed the answer sheet only sporadically although all utilized the space provided for comments. The total number of valid responses was 24.

It was not possible to classify the subjects by sex because some forgot to circle the M/F category on the personal data sheet.

9.5. Analysis

The 38 valid answers were separated by category of raters, personnel employees, and students. The answers for each category to the pertinent questions on each of the two tapes were added together and then compared according to percentiles (von Raffler-Engel et al. 1980b).

9.6. Results

It appears that the more experienced and/or the higher an interviewer is in the corporate scale the keener he is on the assessment of nonverbal factors. Professionals were highly sensitive to variations in nonverbal behavior on the tapes and consistently mentioned 'body language' during our personal meetings. Semi-professionals are almost exclusively oriented towards the verbal message. When asked whether they look at the behavior of the applicant they say that they are 'objective' and try not to be swayed by such 'subjective impressions'. This does not mean that in the reality of the interview situation they are insensitive to nonverbal behavior, it only means that they pay less attention to it than professionals.

While administering the dubbed test I carefully observed the viewers who were semi-professionals. At no time did all of the subjects look at the tape. Some subjects started recording their rating as the tape went on and others continued keeping their head on the paper throughout the first part of the next segment. One subject was so preoccupied with the compilation of the answer sheet that she hardly ever lifted her head to look at the screen. These raters were constantly making the incongruent situation congruent and this was mostly — but by no means always — done in the direction of the verbal component.

The comparison of the ratings for the dubbed and the original tape by the semi-professional personnel workers showed significant results. Incomplete answer sheets were discarded, but on the fourteen completed answer sheets that were utilized there were a few occasional blanks and the numbers on the results are therefore not all 100 percent accurate. In the category 6/a considering whether the raters wanted the applicant as a personal friend, acquaintance, boss, or employee, multiple checkings were possible and did occur on a limited scale.

It appeared that persons working in personnel would hire an applicant who does not exhibit the proper nonverbal behavior if the content of what he says is highly adequate. They would, however, not recommend such a candidate without reservations. The exact tabulation of the answers is provided below.

1. Would you hire the applicant?
   If yes   a)   enthusiastically
            b)   without reservations
            c)   with reservations

dubbed tape poor body, good content	*control* good body, good content
5 no 30 yes	4 no 31 yes
1 a	11 a
19 b	7 b
10 c	13 c

Contrary to the rather limited impact of an applicant's inadequate nonverbal behavior when the content of what he says is excellent, correct nonverbal behavior greatly attenuates the negative impact of an applicant's inappropriate statements.

1. Would you hire the applicant?
   If yes   a)   enthusiastically
            b)   without reservations
            c)   with reservations

dubbed tape good body, poor content	*control* poor body, poor content
20 no 15 yes	33 no 2 yes
1 a	0 a
2 b	1 b
12 c	1 c

The attenuating effect of good body behavior is particularly evident when the subjects decided to fully reject an applicant. While the category for 'never to have anything to do with the applicant outside of professional considerations' was checked only eight (8) times on the tape showing the poor content with the good behavior, it was checked twenty (20) times in reference to the applicant who talked poorly and also behaved poorly.

The same positive effect of body behavior on poor speech content is true, albeit to a lesser degree, for judgment of competence.

5. Does the applicant appear
    a) highly competent
    b) adequately competent
    c) incompetent

dubbed tape poor body, good content	*control* good body, good content
15 a	11 a
20 b	24 b
0 c	0 c

dubbed tape good body, poor content	*control* poor body, poor content
1 a	1 a
23 b	14 b
11 c	20 c

Given the above, the rating of intelligence appears rather puzzling. An applicant whose content of speech is poor but who behaves very properly is rated more frequently of below average intelligence than one whose verbal and body behavior is more consistent.

2. The applicant's intellectual ability is
    a) outstanding
    b) average
    c) below average

dubbed tape poor body, good content	*control* good body, good content
16 a	14 a
17 b	21 b
2 c	0 c

dubbed tape good body, poor content	*control* poor body, poor content
3 a	2 a
17 b	16 b
15 c	7 c

The intelligence rating is the more puzzling when compared to the rating for emotional stability where the discrepancy between verbal and nonverbal behavior influenced rater judgment only slightly.

4. Does the applicant appear emotionally stable?

dubbed tape poor body, good content	*control* good body, good content
2 no 33 yes	0 no 35 yes

dubbed tape good body, poor content	*control* poor body, poor content
12 no 22 yes	10 no 25 yes

The judgment on whether an applicant appears self-reliant, insecure, or overbearing was entirely based on what he said and, surprisingly, unrelated to his nonverbal behavior.

3. The applicant appears
   a) self-reliant
   b) insecure
   c) overbearing

dubbed tape poor body, good content	*control* good body, good content
31 a	32 a
4 b	2 b
0 c	2 c

dubbed tape	*control*
good body, poor content	poor body, poor content
3 a	6 a
24 b	13 b
7 c	11 c
	One subject wrote five
	times 'coddled'.

The results indicate that for semi-professional judges the content of what is said is far more important than nonverbal behavior, but that good body behavior will somewhat smooth the edge when an applicant does not speak properly.

9.7. *Conclusions*

In examining the relationship of verbal and nonverbal factors in the perception of an individual, it means that when the content of an individual's speech is very good, he will be primarily heard while the visual image he presents becomes secondary and is even rationalized to suit the vocal image. Judges of the dubbed tape with the poor body and the good content remarked in their comments that "The applicant seemed to be highly able and competent – at times demonstrating some nervousness, but generally relaxed and at ease." – "Applicant appeared secure, knowledgeable in the beginning ... In the closing scene his body language suggested some insecurity, 'wanting to please'." – "Seemed knowledgeable, but talked with hand over mouth – closed arms, became defensive." In reality, when portraying the poor job applicant, Prof. Dickson was more aggressive than defensive.

To a much lesser degree the tendency to rationalize body behavior to match verbal behavior was present also in the comments by the judges of the dubbed tape with the good body and the poor content. "Applicant was ill-prepared for interview – no background of company – insecure body language and verbal ability." The verbal ability in actuality corresponded to Mr. Spohn's highly professional presentation.

Students of human interaction have long known that people tend to make an incongruent situation congruent. What needs further research is the direction in which the double bind is made congruent. This may vary with the setting (interview, meeting with old friend, classroom interaction, etc.) and also with the degree of positive and negative 'strength' of the verbal, vocal, and nonverbal components of the double bind. In the case of the present study, the setting seems to require congruity in the direction of the verbal component. The same direction is suggested by the 'strength' of the verbal message which was excellent where the nonverbal component was only mildly negative. It remains to be determined at what point the 'strength' of one component may outweigh the requirements of the setting, and vice versa.

In conclusion, the results indicate that in face-to-face interaction one cannot automatically assign a fixed percentage of importance to the verbal, vocal, and nonverbal component. The impact of each of these varies depending on the setting and on the relative strength of each. When the impact of the verbal component is very strong, the nonverbal component becomes secondary and when the impact of the nonverbal component is very strong the verbal component becomes secondary. In the normal attempt to make a non-congruent situation congruent, the attempt will be made in the direction of the more pronounced of the two components.

In the cases of double bind where the conflict between the verbal and the nonverbal component is not overly strong, the direction of congruency stabilizing favors the verbal component. Mildly negative body behavior has only limited impact on the overall rating of an individual with positive verbal behavior. Poor verbal behavior on the contrary has a strong impact on the overall rating of an individual with fairly good behavior.

It is possible that the tendency to make an incongruent situation congruent is not a sociolinguistic universal. It may vary with populations and may be restricted to certain expectancies which depend on the background of the raters. Persons working in personnel may be conditioned to see job applicants as coherent individuals, particularly in view of the fact that this facilitates their task of categorizing these applicants in a standard manner. Nobody suggested that the applicants seen on the dubbed tape were schizophrenics in need of a psychiatrist. The students, however, came close to seeing the contradiction: "Seemed to know material, but weird." "He is incompetent, he is faking it and is probably a bellboy in actuality." Undergraduate students who are young and who have nothing at stake when judging an interviewee may be totally open-minded and look at the videotape in a manner dissimilar from personnel officers. It is unfortunate that time did not permit me to replicate the exact same experiment with a group of professional interviewers.

As I was intrigued by the unanswered question of the strength of the two modalities, I wanted to find out at what point the nonverbal component would be so strong as to overwhelm the impression gained from the verbal component. This time I used truly professional interviewers as judges but I do not have parallel results from students and semi-professionals. In my meetings with executives I observed that the latter are far more cognizant of nonverbal factors than are persons untrained in the art of evaluating people for job qualifications. The results of the test are, nevertheless, highly significative in their own right.

(a) *The instrument* I prepared five frames of a short videotape when an administrator from Vanderbilt University impersonated an interviewer seated across a large wooden desk from a job applicant impersonated by a student. The student wore an open shirt and no jacket but was well-groomed. Except for his 'inappropriate' attire he looked like a young man ready to be interviewed. He spoke with good enunciation and in his statements followed the speech model established by Mr. Spohn on the business school training tape which I mentioned earlier. In his nonverbal behavior, in contrast, he was highly objectionable albeit never to the point of absurdity so that the performance looked always natural. He squirmed on his chair, fidgeted, and rubbed his eyes with his hands and twice even covered his mouth with his hands, looked around in the air establishing only minimal eye contact, and repeatedly played with the telephone cord.

(b) *Subjects, resting procedures, and analysis* The tape was evaluated by seven persons professionally involved in the hiring of lower management personnel in a large hotel in Nashville, Tennessee. Four were male and three were female. The evaluators compiled the same rating sheets I used throughout this study (see Appendix I and II). The answers were compiled in the same statistical manner as for the dubbed tape and all my other experiments.

(c) *Results* In their perception of the applicant, these judges, too, transformed the incongruent situation into a congruent one. In this instance they forced the verbal mode into the nonverbal one. The applicant made very intelligent statements and certainly did not make grammatical mistakes. Two raters, nevertheless, commented negatively on his speech. "Seems intelligent but has a lot of difficulty expressing his views." "Used poor grammar on several occasions." Most revealing was one comment: "The applicant squirmed so much I didn't listen to what he said." He was not hired.

10. DIFFERENCES IN THE PERCEPTION OF NONVERBAL BEHAVIOR AMONG STUDENTS AND NON-STUDENTS AND DEPENDING ON THE SEX AND THE AGE OF THE RATER

The research reported in the preceding chapter revealed that attention to nonverbal cues in the interview situation is not the same for semi-professionals as it is for professional interviewers. Variation in the perception of nonverbal behavior across different groups has not yet received adequate treatment in the kinesic literature.

Much thought has been devoted to cross-cultural differences in nonverbal behavior but intra-cultural divergences between intended and perceived meaning of one and the same kinesic expression have been given little, if any, attention so far. The notable exception is French (1973, 1979) who showed that in-group and same-age raters are better interpreters of gestural behavior than are out-group raters.

An enormous amount of psychological research has been conducted with undergraduates sitting in their college classrooms. With the tacit assumption that the responses of such a captive audience of young people could be generalized to the population at large, nobody ever compared the data obtained in the classroom setting with data from adults under less artificial circumstances. I decided a long time ago that I wanted to challenge the common generalization and with this in mind I approached the research on the interview using non-students as subjects and eventually comparing the results with compatible results obtained from student subjects.

Differences in the language production of men and women have received extensive coverage, mainly in the area of women's language and the language of men about women. The differences in language perception depending on sex have received less attention. With regard to kinesics accurate research is rare, although it is commonplace to assert that women are more sensitive than men to nonverbal cues. Leaving out of consideration mixed-sex communication which has an avowed flirtatious or sexual connotation, one of the fundamental questions in kinesic research that has barely been touched is whether people have a greater facility in correctly interpreting the nonverbal behavior of their own sex as compared to that of the other sex. When describing the gestural motions of third parties, it appears that people tend to identify more readily with their own sex (von Raffler-Engel and Weinstein 1977).

To find out whether students and non-students and males and females reacted the same or differently in the evaluation of nonverbal behaviors I conducted the following test with the valuable assistance of my student Frank Gantz (von Raffler-Engel 1980b; von Raffler-Engel and Gantz 1981).

10.1. *Instrument*

A videotape of the total duration of slightly more than ten minutes was prepared showing five clips depicting a business interview. The words spoken by the interviewer (impersonated by Dr. John Lippincott of the Vanderbilt University Development Office) and his nonverbal behavior remained constant as did the setting across a table. The words spoken by the job applicant (impersonated by Mr. Robin Foster of the Vanderbilt University Learning Resources Center) also remained constant, but his nonverbal behavior varied with each clip.

The verbal part was modeled after the Training Tape prepared by the Owen Graduate School of Management mentioned earlier. The two parties to be taped were asked to memorize the following script:

Interviewer: Andy, you've made a careful job, I think, of filling out your application, but there is other information I'd like to find out about you. How did you find out about Genesco?

Applicant: Well, I've done a great deal of research in our library and I've reviewed the Standard and Poor's and the Moody's Index on your financial position. Aah, I've also done some reading in the Fortune article which was published last summer. I've had an opportunity to meet Mr. Larry Shelton, your vice-chairman, at a seminar which we conducted. I've read your publications and noted who your officials were and their duties. So, I feel I have some understanding of the problems you've been having over the past few years. For instance, as the result of a strong period of acquisition in the 60's, uh, you got to the point where you had more than you could manage; There was a management revolt if you wish to characterize it as such. I'm sure that was overplayed in the media, but there was a distinctive change in the style of management. My own background is in organizational psychology and I've worked with corporate officials trying to help them understand what happens within corporations from a psychological point of view.

The nonverbal behavior in this 'Five Categories tape' varied as follows:

In frame I (Overgesticulation)	The applicant gesticulated almost constantly while he talked, most striking being a pointing gesture with fully extended forearm. The most disturbing feature of this behavior was the lack of normal intra-gestural pauses.
In frame II (Lack of Eye Contact)	The applicant established eye contact with the interviewer only once, looking down or in the air most of the time.
In frame III (Aggressiveness)	The applicant is aggressive, leaning over the table to the limit of his territorial range, facing the interviewer directly most of the time. Gesticulation was minimal.
In frame IV (Fidgeting)	The applicant fidgeted almost constantly, used frequent self-adaptors, and at one point played with the telephone cord.
In frame V (Moderate Aggressiveness)	The applicant is moderately aggressive, leaning slightly forward in a polite posture, with eye contact and moderate gesticulation. The original direction given to the actor had only been to behave as best as he saw fit.

It was decided to have one and the same person act as the job applicant throughout the five frames in order to avoid interference from personality factors. On the other hand, using an identical actor might produce the halo effect introducing bias from the previous impressions on the tape. We opted for the identical person solution believing that this was the lesser of two sources of interferences beyond control.

The five frames were kept to slightly over one minute in duration each. There are three reasons for the time limit. The main reason was that officers in employment agencies and interviewers in business corporations had previously told me that they generally make up their mind within the first few minutes and very rarely change that first impression. A second reason was the observed fact that raters get bored with long tests and chances would be increased that they would not be fully attentive when evaluating the last frames of the series. The third reason is inherent in the perception of nonverbal behavior per se. Specific types of nonverbal behavior cannot be isolated for emphasis and protracted beyond a short time lest they risk looking like a nervous tic, or even lose all sense of naturalness. Unless portrayed by a professional actor (an expensive solution) command performances can hold out only for so long.

10.2. *Testing procedure*

All five video frames were shown to the raters in their numbered sequence and during a single session. After viewing each frame the raters had one minute to compile an identical forced-choice rating sheet consisting of six multiple-choice questions which was the same I used throughout my various research projects (see Appendix I).

10.3. *Subjects*

Through the courtesy of Mr. Lee Binkley, President of the Nashville Chapter of the Industrial Personnel Association of America, I showed the videotape to thirty-seven members of that association during their meeting on Ocober 2, 1979. After the test each rater was requested to mark the rating sheet with M or F for his sex, with a number indicating his age, followed by another number indicating his years of experience in personnel. After elimination of incomplete questionnaires, 28 subjects (21 male and 7 female) remained suitable for study.

This group of professionals was matched for number and sex by undergraduate students who were tested in the same manner by Frank Gantz in a social room at Vanderbilt University. None of the students had ever taken a course in nonverbal behavior. With the exception of one student, none had ever interviewed people for full- or part-time jobs. Some had interviewed other students for fraternity rush, student government positions, or as freshmen counselors. It can be said that the students had no professional experience. Most had themselves been interviewed two to five times, mostly for summer jobs.

The total subject population yielded the following factorial design:

	Males	Females	
Professionals:	24-65	24-57	Age range
	39.2	37.5	Mean age
	½-37	3-20	Years of experience
Students:	18-21	17-21	Age range
	19.6	18.5	Mean age

10.4. *Analysis*

The answers to each question were added together separately for the males and the females. The comparison was established through percentiles calculated with the equivalence of ratios. This was done by hand by my student

Frank Gantz III. In addition, to see whether age and experience among the professional raters were significant variables Noel Lim performed a linear regression analysis by computer.

10.5. Results

10.5.1. Age differences among interviewers

The age of the interviewer had a significative influence on his general attitude towards hiring the applicant. As frames I and II were rated negatively on the whole, there was not much point in examining raters' responses on whether they would or would not hire the applicant. I concentrated on frames III, IV, and V. A linear regression was performed for the total population (See below). As age increased so did the amount of negative responses to question 1.

AGE AND YEARS OF EXPERIENCE OF PROFESSIONAL RATERS

Linear regression analysis of question (hire/not hire)
frames III, IV, and V

Using Ordinary Least Squares (OLS), the following regressions were run:

iii) $H3 = a0 + a1\ AGE + a2\ EXP + e3$

iv) $H4 = b0 + b1\ AGE + b2\ EXP + e4$

v) $H5 = c0 + c1\ AGE + c2\ EXP + e5$

where $a0, b0, c0$ = constant terms

a_i, b_i, c_i = coefficients ($i = 1, 2$)

e_j = error terms ($J = 3, 4, 5$)

H_j = percent of hirers within each age bracket

AGE = midpoint age of age bracket. Brackets used were 24-25, 26-29, 30-33, 34-39, 40-43, 44-49, 50-60, 60 + years of age. Subdivisions were dictated more by the availability of data than considerations of a priori theory.

Thus, H_j are the dependent variables assumed to be linearly dependent on AGE and EXPERIENCE.

The results are reported as follows. T-statistics are in parentheses below each coefficient (T-statistics indicate the significance of the coefficients — coefficients significant at alpha - .05 are marked by a *, those at alpha = .01 by a **). R^2 shows the goodness of fit on the equation — the closer to 1.0, the better the fit. Note the exceptionally good R^2 for H3. SE (Standard Error of the regression) shows the dispersion of the regression coefficients.

iii) $H_3 = 135.220 - 1.411 \text{ AGE} + .089 \text{ EXP} \quad R^2 = .7911$

$\quad\quad\quad (5.578) \quad (-1.442)** \quad\quad (.0556) \quad\quad SE = 11.469$

iv) $H_4 = 57.5101 - 1.883 \text{ AGE} + 3.584 \text{ EXP} \quad R^2 = .2175$

$\quad\quad\quad (1.184) \quad (-.936) \quad\quad\quad (1.116) \quad\quad SE = 22.9754$

v) $H_5 = 159.98 - 2.713 \text{ AGE} + 2.4756 \text{ EXP} \quad R^2 = .5793$

$\quad\quad\quad (3.949) \quad (-1.66)* \quad\quad\quad (.724) \quad\quad SE = 19.165$

The results indicate that as interviewers grow older, the percentage of *not* hiring increases.

Experience apparently has no signficant effect on the hire/not hire decision.

The general trend holds true for both sexes. The seven professional women answered in the following manner:

Age of Rater	No. that would hire	No. that would not hire
24	2	3
25	2	3
29	2	3
37	3	2
40	2	3
50	0	5
57	1	4

The potential for years of experience is obviously related to chronological age, but as people change jobs there is no absolute correlation between an interviewer's age and his years of experience in personnel. Experience was therefore included in the linear regression analysis. Years of experience proved not to be a significant variable. None of the people with whom I met personally was aware of the latter. Many people were, however, aware of the direct relation which obtains between age and severity of judgment. Some attributed it to "experience which makes people more observant" while one young women put it more bluntly: "The older they get the meaner they become."

10.5.2. *Professionals versus students* (see Chart I at end of chapter)

With regard to the hierarchy of nonverbal behavior the result of the new test using a sequence of variations in nonverbal behavior support the results obtained from the previous test using the dubbed videotape. They also confirmed the results from the forced-choice questionnaire administered to campus recruiters from industry by Elizabeth Battey. The one behavior which will adversely affect even an otherwise best qualified applicant is lack of eye contact, and the general body behavior expected of a successful candidate is one of self-control coupled with forceful aggressiveness. On the question of hiring the applicant, Frame II (lack of eye contact) received the largest amount of negative ratings throughout; and Frames III and V (leaning forward moderately or extensively towards the interviewer) received the largest amount of positive ratings.

The use of the new instrument also confirmed that in less clear-cut instances professional judgment diverges from the judgment of raters with different backgrounds.

Insecurity is linked with poor eye contact (Frame II) and fidgeting (Frame III) by both students and professionals, but more students (61%) link this also with emotional instability than do professionals (50%). Professionals (52%) were more apt to label an applicant as incompetent than were students (21%). Students never ranked the applicant as below average in intelligence while professionals did so almost 10% of the time (15 times out of a possible 140).

On the overall, students are more lenient in their assessment of the applicant throughout the various categories. Dipboye *et al.* (1975) compared the evaluation of written resumés by professionals and students and equally concluded that students tended to rate more favorably but otherwise found no basic differences between the groups. Hakel *et al.* (1970a), also looking at the reaction to written resumés by professionals and students, found variation within and between groups in regard to both favorability and content. In the comparisons I performed of the ratings of nonverbal features by professionals and students, I found variation between the groups in regard to both favorability and content. As my data below show, a basic difference can nevertheless be discerned between the performance evaluation by professionals and by students.

It is possible that students identify with the applicant who is only slightly older than they are and that they identify with the person seeking employment as this is eventually what they will do when they finish their schooling. The similar-to-me effect appears to be operant.

In particular, students seem more sympathetic to a nervous applicant. More than double the amount of students would hire the fidgeting applicant in frame IV than would the professionals.

Professionals	yes -	5	no - 23
Students	yes -	11	no - 17

Frame I (excessive gesticulation) produced almost completely opposite results. Only two professional out of 28 would hire the applicant, while among an equal number of 28 students, 22 would hire him. According to the hierarchy survey, a certain amount of appropriate gesticulation may be viewed as 'forcefulness' by professional interviewers and is considered positive, particularly in candidates considered for sales jobs. When gesticulation becomes excessive, however, it is considered 'overbearing' by 79% (n.22) of the professionals and 61% (n.17) of the students. It is possible that students judge less severely because they are less conscious of the implications of such behavior within the hierarchical structure of corporations.

My hypothesis that the perception of an identical behavior will depend on the background of the perceiver was confirmed. The answers to Category 2 (intellectual capability is (a) outstanding; (b) average; (c) below average) showed that college students tend to associate intelligence with hiring in a clear relationship treating a job application as if it were a term paper or a final examination. They do not conceive of a highly intelligent individual being rejected for a job. Albeit they will not hire a person with below average intelligence, professionals do not hesitate to admit that a candidate is of superior or average intelligence but unsuitable for a position.

The most salient difference between students and professionals is in the behavior of the women. Among students men and women react in a very similar fashion while among professionals the behavior of the women is distinct from that of the men.

10.5.3. *Comparison by sex – Professionals* (See Chart II at end of chapter)

In comparing the responses by sex, three differences became apparent. Although basically men and women agree on whether an applicant should be hired, women tend to be slightly more severe in their ratings. By summing up the yes/no replies to the question of whether an applicant should be hired, the following chart is obtained:

M yes	M no	F yes	F no
2	19	0	7
3	18	0	7
16	5	6	1
4	17	1	6
16	5	5	2
41	64	12	25

To establish the equivalence of ratios between the 21 male and 7 female respondents, the total female responses must be multiplied by 3 obtaining a ratio among the M and F totals of:

M   yes - 41;   F   yes - 36
M   no - 64;   F   no - 75

This shows that the women are approximately 15% more critical of the candidate than the men.

I discussed these findings with Prof. Samuel Richmond, Dean of the Owen Graduate School of Management at Vanderbilt University, who was not at all surprised. He believes that it is not that women in general are more severe judges than men, but that the type of women that goes into management is temperamentally more captious than other women and professionally constantly aware of the fact that she must excel if she wants to compete in a man's world. Prof. Robert Ullrich, the associate dean of the Owen Graduate School of Management also told me that the GPA and the test scores of the female applicants for the MBA program consistently exceed those of the male applicants to the program. Women who go into business careers are extremely competitive in orientation.

Looking at specific types of nonverbal behavior the following differences according to the sex of the rater were detected. When rating frame IV depicting the fidgeting candidate, among the professional women 85% felt that the candidate was not emotionally stable, while among the men only 50% judged in this manner. On the overall, however, the women are not significantly different from their male counterparts when it comes to deciding whether or not to hire the applicant. The female ratings are only slightly more negative. Frame IV Question 1 produced the following results adjusted to the equivalence of ratios:

Hire	Not Hire
M 4	M 17
F 3	F 18

That women are more irritated than men by a fidgeting candidate was also confirmed by the survey questionnaire which had been administered to campus recruiters from industry at the Vanderbilt University Career Planning and Placement Office. Pearson's multiple correlation test showed that sex was significantly correlated to the nonverbal feature of fidgeting. I talked with several personnel executives about their attitude towards nervous fidgeting. The majority of the women told me that it makes them nervous and they could not personally work with such a person but others usually can. The men were less affected by fidgeting and said that a candidate, particularly when he is young and inexperienced, is apprehensive in the interview situation and they would not hold it against him in the first interview. In a second interview they would consider such behavior in relation to the job requirements. An accountant in a back office would be judged differently from a salesman that has to inspire confidence. For men, thus, the impact of fidgeting was viewed in relation to an employee's public image. Otherwise it was considered not too important an expression of his personality.

Boyle *et al.* (1980) report that in his dissertation Sterrett (1976) found that "male managers reacted positively to 'excess body language', whereas female managers reacted negatively." Neither Boyle *et al.* nor Sterrett (1976, 1978) specify whether they distinguish clearly between hand gesticulation and fidgeting. It may simply indicate that women react negatively to fidgeting.

The difference between men and women judges is also apparent when comparing the results from frame III and frame V. These two frames were not ostensibly strongly dissimilar like all the other frames. In both frames basically the candidate did all the proper things, he did nothing blantantly wrong like in all the other frames. The two frames differ in the following manner: in frame V the candidate is assertive while in frame III he is slightly aggressive, leaning forward on the desk.

While all the personnel managers preferred the more aggressive candidate, the preference is very slight among the males but it is pronounced among the females. The latter find him more intelligent and more competent. Where the women differ most is on Question 3. The female raters — with the exception of one who systematically ranked both frames in the lowest manner possible — rated only the aggressive candidate as self-reliant considering the non-aggressive candidate in frame V as insecure. The vast majority of male raters considered both candidates self-reliant. A few men considered both candidates insecure or overbearing. In this particular frame V (control) the young man impersonating the applicant was told to behave completely naturally as he would in a regular interview situation He had had a total of six interviews during his life with a 60% success rate. The only instruction he was given was to try as much as possible to avoid gestures he had used in the previous frames. He later told me that he had a slight hesitancy at a certain point and this extremely brief instance of indecision may have been detected by the female judges. This could possibly confirm that "women may be more sensitive to other's emotional states than men" (Weitz 1976; Halle 1978, reported in Weitz 1979: 32), but I will come to this later.

On the overall, from my research data it cannot be ascertained whether the candidates rejected by the female raters are actually of inferior quality or simply exhibit some forms of behavior which elicit negative reactions in women. Provided that the objectionable behaviors are indeed indicative of lack of qualifications for the job, the reason for women's more critical approach to the evaluation of nonverbal behavior could be either innate or learned. The two alternatives are as follows:

(a) All women are innately more powerfully equipped to understand nonverbal behavior because
  (i) they are more perceptive; or
  (ii) they instinctively work harder at uncovering the real self of an interlocutor.

(b) Those who choose business careers constitute a special group of women, viz.
  (i) they are temperamentally more captious; or
  (ii) they simply are constantly on the alert to compete in what traditionally is a man's work.

When I mentioned to personnel executives that the statistical analysis of a forced-choice questionnaire showed that male and female interviewers agree in extreme situations but vary greatly in their evaluaton of diverse nonverbal cues I received a great disparity of replies. Many men were genuinely surprised at the findings while all women said that they knew this all along. Most women asserted that they are "the stronger sex and innately more sensitive and more clever". A minority of women believed in the power theory of sex differences and considered it a learned response albeit one that after so many generations of subordination could have become genetically conditioned. The men were about equally divided into those who believed that women are instinctively "more perceptive and more cunning" and those who feel that only women who are temperamentally high strung go into personnel work.

My own findings would concur with the second alternative. A comparison of male and female student responses to the same tapes that were shown to the personnel professionals showed no appreciable difference along sex lines although there were differences when comparing the students and the professionals as a group. It does therefore seem that the type of woman who goes into management is temperamentally more captious than other women and professionally constantly aware of the fact that she must be extremely competitive in orientation. It would be important to perform a follow-up test with a large number of female students divided by their career goals to determine whether the women who plan to go into business react differently from those who have other career goals.

10.4.5. *Comparison by sex – Students* (See Chart III at end of chapter)

Male and female students can hardly be distinguished when it comes to hiring an applicant. The total of female yes answers is 25 and the males' total is 74. Once the equivalence of ratios is established the relationship is 75:74. How many, if any, of the women students plan to go into management careers cannot be ascertained. In subsequent tests of this sort such a question will be included in the personal data sheet.

The slight moment of hesitancy in frame V was detected by 50% more male students than women students:

F   yes - 4 (=12)   F   no - 3 (=9)
M   yes - 8   M   no - 13

This makes one wonder whether women are biologically more perceptive than men or whether they became more perceptive as culture forces them into harsher realities with regard to their careers. It is conceivable that in this particular instance males had a clearer perception of same-sex behavior.

The most intriguing finding is that undergraduate women do not at all react to fidgeting like professional women do. Frame IV elicited more negative replies from men than from women concerning the hiring of the fidgeting applicant.

F   yes - 4 (equivalent to 12)   M   yes - 7
F   no - 3 ("   "   9)   M   no - 14

The difference among professional women and women students is likely to be due to the combination of their young age and the fact that they are not professionals. It may also be that being students who eventually have to undergo the pains of an interview, they are more sympathetic to the nervousness of the young man. Why male students would be less sympathetic is not clear unless there is a tendency for more lenience in other-sex judgments than in same-sex judgments.

That the latter might be a possibility would be supported by the fact that more men than women were critical of the moment of hesitancy in frame V explored above. One could conclude that professionals are more distant from their subjects than raters who do not feel obliged to make a concerted effort to keep all emotional involvement under control. Neither severity nor leniency, of course, are necessarily related to degree of awareness. My results neither contradict nor give conclusive support to the common belief mentioned on page 92 that "women may be more sensitive to other's emotional states than men (Weitz 1976; Hall 1978, reported in Weitz 1979: 32).

If alternative (a) (see page 93) is correct and women are natively more sensitive to nonverbal factors or innately geared to probe deeper into the real self of others, either instinct must be released at a later date, either automatically by age, or by certain circumstances. It is not apparent in students but fully present in professional women. Such an hypothesis might get support from the research by Buck (1975) albeit the latter examined the sender and not the receiver and children rather than young adults. In the research conducted by this author, sex differences in the capability of sending nonverbal signals of emotion cannot be detected in children but are manifest in adults. Buck attributes the developmental difference to socialization.

If alternative (b) (see page 93) is correct, particularly (ii) that women are more careful and afraid to make a wrong decision in hiring an employee, it is possible that such extraordinary precaution no longer applies to the new generation where women have begun to feel accepted as equals in the world of business.

10.5.5. *Comparison by sex – All males versus all females* (See Charts IV, V, and VI at end of chapter)

With regard to a comparison of all males versus all females in the sample, I am not confident that the results would be of value. Given that the behavior of the female students did not differ essentially from that of the male students, but that the professionals were clearly distinguished by sex, an overall comparison becomes problematic within a limited size population.

What my research indicates is that professional women consciously attribute a greater degree of importance to nonverbal behavior than their male counterparts. Towards the end of the Hierarchy Survey Questionnaire (see chart in chapter 5), the respondents were asked to rate on a scale from 0 to 9 how much weight they placed on the nonverbal behaviors that had been listed above in comparison to a person's skills and background. Of the female campus recruiters, one forgot to circle any number and of the 24 males one circled no number and wrote in margin "depends on job". Both replies were considered void, reducing the number of valid responses to 5 women and 23 men. One man did not circle any number and wrote "almost none". His answer was counted as ½ point. One man circled (5 - 6) and his number was counted as 5½. The distribution of points of relative weight thus emerged as follows:

F(5)		M(23)	
No. of subjects	Weight	No. of subjects	Weight
		1	$^1/_2$
		1	1
		3	3
		2	4
1	5	4	5
		1	$5^1/_2$
2	6	1	6
		6	7
1	8	3	8
1	8+	1	9
MEAN 6.6		MEAN 5.4	

The mean weight strongly favors the women. Most indicative is the fact that the women have not a single response in the lower ranks. The median, thus, indicates even more strongly that women recruiters admittedly give more importance to nonverbal behavior than men.

The Five Categories video study had 21 men and 7 women giving a ratio of 1:3 and the survey questionnaire had 24 men and 6 women giving a ratio of 1:4. These numbers speak for themselves concerning the proportion of men and women who make personnel decisions but are not ideal for a comparative study on sex differences. In the Five Categories video study it would have been relatively easy to ask a sufficient number of undergraduate women to come to the Vanderbilt University Learning Resources Center to view the testing tape, but it was absolutely beyond the time available to either myself or Frank Gantz III to ask 14 women in industrial personnel offices to come to the university at variable times of their convenience, not to mention the alternative of carrying the video equipment to a series of plants.

In the Survey Questionnaire these were all the campus recruiters Elizabeth Battey was able to contact at the Vanderbilt Career and Placement Service before the end of the recruiting season. We could have given the questionnaire to 18 women recruiters during the subsequent season, but Battey graduated and my other student, Jeffrey Rothschild who did the analysis, received his M.A. in Computer Science and left for a lucrative job in Arizona.

If not conclusive, my findings are certainly indicative of sex differences and I hope some reader will find a way to continue this type of research with controlled cells. Both men and women to whom I mentioned the difference during my meetings with business executives were astonished at these facts. They all believed that male and female iterviewers would look at the candidate in the same fashion. Basically they are right because the difference in approach is one of degree and not of kind.

During my personal meetings with executives we talked at length about women and minority candidates. There is no difference in how men and women view minorities, but there is a difference depending on whether the interviewer and the interviewee are of the same sex or not. All interviewers agree that they look for the same type of aggressive and capable person in men as well as women candidates, and that they measure the nonverbal behavior of both sexes in the same manner. Women interviewers are generally slightly more comfortable with men candidates than men interviewers are with opposite sex candidates. Men sometimes find it difficult to shake hands with female applicants at the completion of the interview. This is one area where they judge nonverbal behavior differently. A hearty handshake is expected from a male candidate and 'fishy' handshakes definitely create a negative impression. In those instances that handshakes occur between men interviewers and female candidates, "it does not matter how she gives her hand".

During interviews which I have observed in vivo male interviewers kept a slightly larger inter-personal distance between themselves and the applicant when the latter was a woman. When leaning forward they also did this to a lesser extent. Across the table vis-a-vis settings were not affected, but the spatial arrangement was sex-specific when it took place in the side-by-side setting. Many interviews start across a desk or a conference table and then move to the less formal seating arrangement on two armchairs.

Men interviewers mention that attempts by female candidates to use sex to improve their job ratings achieve exactly the opposite effect. Women interviewers do not seem to think that male applicants could make similar attempts. A very unusual sex manipulation on the part of the interviewer was reported in one of our personal meetings by Mrs. Gail Larson who owns an employment agency. As the labor market in nursing is highly competitive, a very attractive young male recruiter was utilized to interview prospective nurses for a major hospital.

Concerning an applicant's clothing, sex is only mentioned for women by both male and female interviewers. "The hiring of women differs from that of men because physical attractiveness plays a major role in the public image" said a personnel executive in one of our meetings. From this it would appear that women are judged more intensely than men on their general appearance.

They are also classified depending on what they wear. Women in business suits are perceived as fitting into an office while women in fashionable attire are considered for sales jobs. Men are scrutinized for neatness and suit and tie is preferred, but the style of the suit and the color of the tie are hardly noticed. For women it is assumed that they express a great deal of their personality and attitudes in the type of clothes they select. Wearing apparel, thus, carries more weight for women than for men. This seems to be the consensus of both male and female interviewers.

10.6. Conclusion

Given the disparity in numbers between males and females any comparison between the sexes can only be considered indicative rather than conclusive. The results, nevertheless, are significant because they are extremely consistent. My findings also raise a vital issue concerning the severity of judgment associated with women in the context of nonverbal behavior. When confronted with written and strictly verbal information, London and Poplawski (1976: 204) found that "In general, ratings by females were higher than ratings by males." Contrary to this, in the findings I have presented in this chapter and in all my previous research on the impact of the interviewer's sex on his judgment of the nonverbal behavior of a white male applicant, sex proved to be a significant variable and professional women were consistently harsher judges than men. My findings thus contradict all previous research. Boyle et al. (1980) report that Dipboye et al. (1977) found that the sex of the interviewer had no influence on the rating of job candidates and that London and Poplawski (1976) found that women were more lenient in their ratings. The same holds true for London and Hakel (1974). The disparity of results can possibly be explained by two factors. One is that there are clear-cut instances where everybody agrees on hiring or not hiring a candidate while middle-of-the-road candidates seem to be judged more harshly by women than men. The other is that in addition to overall evaluations, my research investigates the reaction to a set of specific categories of nonverbal behavior establishing a hierarchy of such categorization. In these instances, my findings point to differences in kind, beyond differences in degree. In conclusion, my research design is not compatible with the articles in the Journal of Applied Psychology and the data thus cannot be compared.

For a further comparison of male and female responses, see chapter 11, page 110 ff. Men and women do not only differ in their rating of various types of nonverbal behavior. It also makes a difference whether men or women rate same-sex or other-sex subjects.

The results from my multiple design approach concord in pointing to consistent differences depending on the sex, the age, and the background of the rater.

That any nonverbal message is not interpreted unanimously even within the same culture is clear considering that the receiver's perception of the sender's nonverbal behavior is determined by the following three factors:

(a) The socio-cultural expectancies of the receiver which may or may not coincide with those of the sender, either
   (i) basically, or
   (ii) partially.
(b) The definition the receiver has
   (i) of the context and the situation in which the interaction takes place, and
   (ii) of the inter-personal relationship between himself and the sender, and between the sender and other interactants that may be present.
(c) The ego-state of the receiver. The latter is dependent
   (i) on his general health, external conditions (such as weather), and his biological rhythm; and
   (ii) on his mood which is an extension of a state previous to the present moment. The given mood may persist or change at some point during the novel experience of the interaction.

Experienced personnel workers are well aware of the influence of 'the mood of the moment' and try to ask a co-worker to take over important interviews when they do not "feel in the proper condition to make an intelligent desicion". Businesses also train their interviewers to recognize differences in behavioral styles and 'mannerisms' of minorities and people from different social classes. Rating sheets increasingly contain rubrics for 'Appearance: Grooming, posture, dress, manners, and neatness'.

In addition to the above contingency factors of shared presuppositions, assessment of the situation, and mood, face-to-face interactions also involve attributive factors. The evaluation of nonverbal behavior is influenced by conscious and unconscious elements. The rater judges from a base which combines his personality, his language-and-culture background, and his professional training. Nobody is fully cognizant of all his personality traits. An individual's cultural background too has conscious and unconscious elements. Even educational and professional training are not consistently on one's level of awareness. Personnel workers pride themselves in 'being objective' and in their careful appraisal of a job applicant's behavior for which they say they follow learned rules. At the same time, the expression which came up in virtually every meeting I had with professional interviewers was 'gut feeling'. When asked to explain what they meant by 'gut feeling', the definition most frequently was something like 'native aptitude plus experience'.

The following are the five attributive factors involved in the rating of non-verbal behavior.

(a) The kinesic-cultural background of the receiver. He may come
    (i)   from a high-kinesic culture; or
    (ii) from a low-kinesic culture.

People have a selective perception of body movements. Persons from high-kinesic cultures see movements which persons from low-kinesic cultures do not appear to notice (von Raffler-Engel *et al.* 1978).

(b) Personality traits of the receiver. He may be
    (i)   a high self-monitoring individual, or
    (ii) a low self-monitoring indivudal.

According to Snyder (1980) high self-monitoring individuals carefully tailor their behavior to match the occasion while low self-monitoring individuals are less concerned about what impression they make on others. The former are also considerably more adept at seeing through deceptive appearances and able to detect insincerity. One of the purposes of the stress interview is to put the candidate off-guard in order to reveal his true self. Top professional interviewers distinguish between the real self, the self image (what the person thinks of himself), the projected images (the impression a person makes on others), and the attempted image (the impression he wants to make on others).

(c) The sex of the receiver:
    (i)   his own, male or female;
    (ii) and in relation to the sender, same-sex or other-sex.

(d) The age of the receiver,
    (i)   his own; and
    (ii) in relation to the age of the sender.

(e) The educational background and professional training of the receiver. They may influence his perception
    (i)   because of the general formative impact the latter exert on his judgment; or

(ii) by reason of their specific relation to all or some of the interactants and to the message conveyed by the sender.

The evaluation by professionals and by college students of identical videotaped interview situations showed significative differences in the interpretation of the same movements even when the two groups agreed in the description of these movements. Hakel *et al.* (1970b) compared the contrast effect on professionals and students evaluating written resumés and found very little difference between the groups. Contrast affected just over 1% of the decision making process for professionals and 2% for students. This negligible difference does not necessarily contradict my findings. As a matter of fact, in my sample there are areas of inter-group agreement as well as disagreement. That groups differ does not automatically imply that they differ on everything. It is clear from my research results that the background of the viewer influences his evaluation of nonverbal behavior.

My research was purposely restricted to sub-cultural differences within mainstream America. Even among those, I have only explored the variables of sex, age, professional experience as a career interviewer, and student versus non-student status. Many more variables could – and should – be studied and it is my sincere hope that others will pick up where I left.

Somewhat beyond this study, I wanted to get a general idea of the reaction of people outside the American culture to the same situation. For this purpose I showed the six-frame videotape with the multiple candidates (described in chapter 4) at the Goethe Institute in Munich, Germany, courtesy Dr. Helm von Faber. The subjects were teachers of German as a Foreign Language enrolled in an advanced summer seminar in 1981. All the subjects had a good command of English. The total number of subjects was 24 (11 M/13 F) but two (M) of these were from the United States. The 22 suitable subjects ranged in age from 30 to 35 years and came from the following countries: Algeria 1 (M), Australia 1 (F), Canada 1 (M recently from Switzerland), Denmark 1 (F), England 1 (M), France 4 (2 M/2 F), Greece 1 (F), Italy 2 (F), Iceland 1 (M), Japan 3 (1 M/2 F), Poland 1 (M), Portugal 2 (1 M/1 F), Turkey 1 (F), Yugoslavia 2 (F). I distributed the rating sheets in the usual manner but when I tried to collect them, all the subjects told me that they were unable to fill them out because the situation looked so strange to them that they could not form any judgment.

Chart I

TOTALS (Professionals)		N = 28		Age range = 24-65	
I	II	III	IV	V
1a) 2yes 26no	3yes 25no	22yes 6no	5yes 23no	21yes 7no
b) 1a 1c	1b 2c	2a 13b 7c	1b 4c	2a 10b 9c
2) 5a 20b 3c	4a 20b 4c	12a 14b 2c	3a 21b 4c	7a 19b 2c
3) 6a 22c	1a 17b 4c	23a 2b 3c	3a 23b 3c	16a 7b 5c
4) 15yes 13no	13yes 14no*	24yes 4no	11yes 16no*	24yes 4no
5) 4a 20b 4c	1a 17b 10c	9a 17b 2c	1a 14b 13c	7a 19b 2c
6) 3b 1c 2d 22e	1a 8b 1c 2d 16e	3a 4b 1c 17d 3e	10b 1c 3d 14e	3a 4b 2c 13d 6e

* One subject answered "yes/no". His response is not included.

TOTALS (Students)		N = 28		Age range = 17-21	
I	II	III	IV	V
1a) 22yes 6no	7yes 21no	23yes 5no	11yes 17no	26yes 2no
b) 2a 9b 11c	1b 6c	8a 6b 9c	2b 9c	14a 9b 3c
2) 19a 9b	10a 18b	20a 6b 2c	6a 22b	20a 8b
3) 9a 2b 17c	3a 25b	17a 10b 1c	2a 25b 1c	27a 1c
4) 24yes 4no	12yes 16no	24yes 4no	12yes 16no	28yes
5) 19a 9b	4a 17b 7c	18a 10b	2a 22b 4c	23a 5b
6) 8b 6d 14c	2a 4b 6d 16e	2a 11b 3c 8d 4e	12b 5d 10e	5a 10b 2c 10d 1e

Chart II

MALES (Professionals)		N = 21		Age range = 24-65 ($\overline{X}$=39.2)	
I	II	III	IV	V
1a) 2yes 19no	3yes 18no	16yes 5no	4yes 17no	16yes 5no
b) 1a 1c	1b 2c	2a 8b 6c	4c	2a 8b 6c
2) 5a 13b 3c	4a 15b 2c	9a 11b 1c	3a 14b 4c	7a 13b 1c
3) 6a 15c	1a 17b 3c	17a 2b 2c	2a 17b 2c	16a 1b 4c
4) 10yes 11no	9yes 11no*	18yes 3no	10yes 10no*	18yes 3no
5) 4a 13b 4c	1a 14b 6c	6a 14b 1c	1a 10b 10c	7a 13b 1e
6) 2b 2d 17e	1a 7b 2d 11e	3a 3b 12d 3e	9b 1d 11e	3a 4b 1c 8d 5e

* One applicant answered "yes/no". His response is not included.

FEMALES (professionals)   N = 7   Age range = 24-57 ($\overline{X}$=37.5)

	I	II	III	IV	V
1a)	7no	7no	6yes 1no	1yes 6no	5yes 2no
b)	————	————	5b 1c	1b	2b 3c
2)	7b	5b 2c	3a 3b 1c	7b	6b 1c
3)	7c	6b 1c	6a 1c	1a 6b	6b 1c
4)	5yes 2no	4yes 3no	6yes 1no	1yes 6no	6yes 1no
5)	7b	3b 4c	3a 3b 1c	4b 3c	6b 1c
6)	1b 1c 5e	1b 1c 5e	1b 1c 5d	1b 1c 2d 3e	1c 5d 1e

Chart III
FEMALES (Undergraduates)   N = 7   Age range = 17-21 ($\overline{X}$=18.5)

	I	II	III	IV	V
1a)	6yes 1no	2yes 5no	6yes 1no	4yes 3no	7yes
b)	6b	2c	2a 2b 2c	1b 3a	4a 3b
2)	6a 1b	3a 4b	5a 2c	2a 5b	6a 1b
3)	3a 4c	7b	6a 1c	1a 6b	7a
4)	7yes	4yes 3no	4yes 3no	4yes 3no	7yes
5)	5a 2b	2a 3b 2c	4a 3b	1a 6b	7a
6)	3b 1d 3e	1b 1d 5e	1a 2b 1c 2d 1e	4b 2d 1e	1a 3b 1c 2d

MALES (Undergraduates)   N = 21   Age range = 18-21 ($\overline{X}$=19.6)

	I	II	III	IV	V
1a)	16yes 24no	5yes 16no	17yes 4no	7yes 14no	19yes 2no
b)	2a 3b 11c	1b 4c	6a 4b 7c	1b 6c	10a 6b 3c
2)	13a 8b	7a 14b	15a 6b	14a 7b	14a 7b
3)	6a 2b 13c	3a 18b	11a 9b 1c	1a 19b 1c	20a 1c
4)	17yes 4no	8yes 13no	20yes 1no	8yes 13no	21yes
5)	14a 7b	2a 14b 5c	14a 7b	1a 16b 4c	16a 5b
6)	5b 5d 11c	2a 3b 5d 11c	1a 9b 2c 6d 3e	8b 4d 9e	4a 7b 1c 8d 1e

Chart IV

MALES (Professionals)   N = 21   Age range = 24-65 ($\bar{X}$=39.2)

	I	II	III	IV	V
1a)	2yes 19no	3yes 18no	16yes 5no	4yes 17no	16yes 5no
b)	1a 1c	1b 2c	2a 8b 6c	4c	2a 8b 6c
2)	5a 13b 3c	4a 15b 2c	9a 11b 1c	3a 14b 4c	7a 13b 1c
3)	6a 15c	1a 17b 3c	17a 2b 2c	2a 17b 2c	16a 1b 4c
4)	10yes 11no	9yes 11no*	18yes 3 no	10yes 10no*	18yes 3no
5)	4a 13b 4c	1a 14b 6c	6a 14b 1c	1a 10b 10c	7a 13b 1c
6)	2b 2d 17e	1a 7b 2d 11e	3a 3b 12d 3e	9b 1d 11e	3a 4b 1c 8d 5e

* One subject answered "yes/no". His response is not included.

MALES (Undergraduates)   N = 21   Age range = 18-21 ($\bar{X}$=19.6)

	I	II	III	IV	V
1a)	16yes 5no	5yes 16no	17yes 4no	7yes 14no	19yes 2no
b)	2a 3b 11c	1b 4c	6a 4b 7c	1b 6c	10a 6b 3c
2)	13a 8b	7a 14b	15a 6b	4a 17b	14a 7b
3)	6a 2b 13c	3a 18b	11a 9b 1c	1a 19b 1c	20a 1c
4)	17yes 4no	8yes 13no	20yes 1no	8yes 13no	21yes
5)	14a 7b	2a 14b 5c	14a 7b	1a 16b 4c	16a 5b
6)	5b 5d 11e	2a 3b 5d 11e	1a 9b 2c 6d 3e	8b 4d 9e	4a 7b 1c 8d 1e

Chart V

FEMALES (Professionals)   N = 7   Age range = 24-57 ($\bar{X}$=37.5)

	I	II	III	IV	V
1a)	7no	7no	6yes 1no	1yes 6no	5yes 2no
b)	————	————	5b 1c	1b	2b 3c
2)	7b	5b 2c	3a 3b 1c	7b	6b 1c
3)	7c	6b 1c	6a 1c	1a 6b	6b 1c
4)	5yes 2no	4yes 3no	6yes 1no	1yes 6no	6yes 1no
5)	7b	3b 4c	3a 3b 1c	4b 3c	6b 1c
6)	1b 1c 5e	1b 1c 5e	1b 1c 5d	1b 1c 2d 3e	1c 5d 1e

FEMALES (Undergraduates)   N = 7   Age range = 17-21 ($\bar{X}$=18.5)

	I	II	III	IV	V
1a)	6yes 1no	2yes 5no	6yes 1no	4yes 3no	7yes
b)	6b	2c	2a 2b 2c	1b 3c	4a 3b
2)	6a 1b	3a 4b	5a 2c	2a 5b	6a 1b
3)	3a 4c	7b	6a 1c	1a 6b	7a
4)	7yes	4yes 3no	4yes 3no	4yes 3no	7yes
5)	5a 2b	2a 3b 2c	4a 3b	1a 6b	7a
6)	3b 1d 3e	1b 1d 5e	1a 2b 1c 2d 1e	4b 2d1e	1a 3b 1c 2d

Chart VI

TOTALS (Females)   N = 14

	I	II	III	IV	V
1a)	6yes 8no	2yes 12no	12yes 2no	5yes 9no	12yes 2no
b)	6b	2c	2a 7b 3c	2b 3c	4a 5b 3c
2)	6a 8b	3a 9b 2c	8a 3b 3c	2a 12b	6a 7b 1c
3)	3a 11c	13b 1c	12a 2c	2a 12b	12a 2c
4)	12yes 2no	8yes 6no	10yes 4no	5yes 9no	13yes 1no
5)	5a 9b	2a 6b 6c	7a 6b 1c	1a 10b 3c	7a 6b 1c
6)	4b 1c 1d 8e	2b 1c 1d 10e	1a 3b 1c 7d 2e	5b 1c 4d 4e	1a 3b 2c 7d 1e

TOTALS (Males)   N = 42

	I	II	III	IV	V
1a)	18yes 24no	8yes 34no	33yes 9no	11yes 31no	35yes 7no
b)	3a 3b 12c	2b 6c	8a 12b 13c	1b 10c	12a 14b 9c
2)	18a 21b 3c	11a 29b 2c	24a 17b 1c	7a 31b 4c	21a 20b 1c
3)	12a 2b 28c	4a 35b 3c	28a 2b 11c 1d	3a 36b 3c	36a 1b 5c
4)	27yes 15no	17yes 24no*	38yes 4no	18yes 23no*	39yes 3no
5)	18a 20b 4c	3a 28b 11c	20a 21b 1c	2a 26b 14c	23a 18b 1c
6)	7b 7d 28e	3a 10b 11c 7d 11e	4a 12b 2c 18d 6e	17b 4d 20e	7a 11b 2c 16d 6e

* One subject answered "yes/no". His response is not included.

11. DIFFERENCES IN THE EVALUATION OF NONVERBAL BEHAVIOR DEPENDING ON THE SEX OF THE SENDER

The primary goal of my research is to test for possible variations in the way the receiver of a nonverbal message interprets that message depending on his own background. For a neat research design it was essential to keep the sender of the message constant within an identical situation. The situation was the career interview and the sender was a young male applicant for an opening in junior management. I selected a white male job applicant for three reasons. Firstly, the interviewee in the Management School Training Tape described in chapter 9 was a white man in his mid-twenties and I wanted my new data to be cumulative. Secondly, the interviewer in that same tape was also a white male and I did not want to introduce additional variables by having the two participants differ in sex and/or race. Thirdly, I wanted the situation to look as natural as possible and in today's business world the male applicant is more common than the female job seeker, and white people are in the majority in the United States of America. I am not reinforcing existing prejudices but simply coping with facts.

Having established a pattern of receiver reaction towards the standard candidate, I proceeded to examine the reaction to other candidates, such as white women and minorities. So far, I have held the age factor constant across the various research projects. This chapter examines the perception of nonverbal behavior in the white female job applicant. The personality factor for the male candidate versus the female candidate beyond the sex difference cannot be ascertained. Eventually, several male candidates will be compared with an equal number of female candidates to equalize such influences. I am confident, nevertheless, that the findings are significative. In many ways the test results support standard stereotyping.

11.1. *The rating of a female vs. a male candidate*

Two students of mine, Lisa Collins and Charles Huddleston, became interested in the male/female comparison and did all the work involved in the production of the instrument, the testing, and analysis. Presently they continue working on the project to increase the subject population.

11.1.1. *Instrument*

A videotape sequence was produced consisting of five frames, each lasting slightly over one minute and followed by a minute-long pause to allow for rating time. The tape depicted a white male interviewer and a young white female job applicant. In all segments the setting and the total behavior of the interviewer remained constant while the applicant maintained the same verbal content but varied her nonverbal behavior in the same manner as had the white male applicant described in chapter 10. The frame sequence was thus the same as in the preceding research project outlined in chapter 10, page 85.

For the ease of the reader the frame sequence is shown again below:

In frame I (Overgesticulation)	The applicant gesticulated almost constantly while he talked, most striking being a pointing gesture with fully extended forearm. The most disturbing feature of this behavior was the lack of normal intra-gestural pauses.
In frame II (Lack of Eye Contact)	The applicant established eye contact with the interviewer only once, looking down or in the air most of the time.
In frame III (Aggressiveness)	The applicant is aggressive, leaning over the table to the limit of his territorial range, facing the interviewer directly most of the time. Gesticulation was minimal.
In frame IV (Fidgeting)	The applicant fidgeted almost constantly, used frequent self-adaptors and at one point played with the telephone cord.
In frame V (Moderate Aggressiveness)	The applicant is moderately aggressive, leaning slightly forward in a polite posture, with eye contact and moderate gesticulation. The original direction given to the actor had only been to behave as best as he saw fit.

11.1.2. *Subjects and testing procedure.*

The video sequence was shown to a total of 29 subjects (M 15, age range 30-49 / F 14, age range 22-60+). All subjects had experience in interviewing job applicants. Sixteen were employed at a large hospital in Nashville, Tennessee, nine were managers at the Nissan Corporation in Smyrna, Tennessee, and four were professionals at the Vanderbilt University Library. All compiled the usual personal data and performance rating sheets (see Appendix I and II) within the one minute interval following each frame.

11.1.3. *Results: Rating of female vs. male candidate*

In comparing the responses for the female applicant with those previously obtained for the male applicant, the following results were obtained and are subsequently analyzed for each question.

Comparison of male and female applicant

Female Applicant
Totals (professionals)   N = 29

	I	II	III	IV	V
1a)	14yes 15no	8yes 21no	16yes 13no	9yes 20no	29yes
b)	1a 2b 11c	8c	2a 7b 7c	1b 8c	12a 14b 2c*
2)	20a 9b	9a 19b 1c	15a 14b	7a 22b	20a 9b
3)	8a 21c	29b	21a 1b 7c	29b	29a
4)	22yes 7no	13yes 16no	28yes 1no	12yes 17no	29yes
5)	10a 16b 3c	24b 5c	8a 20b 1c	1a 23b 5c	18a 11b
6)	6b 9d 14e	16b 4d 9e	2a 12b 10d 5e	16b 4d 9e	5a 1b 22d**

* One person omitted the b part.
**One person answered b/d. This response was not included.

Male Applicant
Totals (professionals)   N = 28

	I	II	III	IV	V
1a)	2yes 26no	3yes 25no	22yes 6no	5yes 23no	21yes 7no
b)	1a 1c	1b 20	2a 13b 7c	1b 4c	2a 10b 9c
2)	5a 20b 3c	4a 20b 4c	12a 14b 2c	3a 21b 4c	7a 19b 2c
3)	6a 22c	1a 17b 4c	23a 2b 3c	3a 23b 3c	16a 7b 5c
4)	15yes 13no	13yes 14no	24yes 4no	11yes 16no*	24yes 4no
5)	4a 20b 4c	1a 17b 10c	9a 17b 2c	1a 14b 13c	7a 19b 2c
6)	3b 1c 2d 22e	1a 8b 1c 2d 16e	3a 4b 1c 17d 3e	10b 1c 3d 14e	3a 4b 2c 13d 6e

* One person answered "yes/no". His response is not included.

Comparison of male and female applicant

Question 1: Would you hire the applicant? A) yes no B) if yes, a) enthusiastically b) without reservations c) with reservations

Frame I: Overgesticulation

	female			male		
a)	yes		no	yes		no
	48.3%		51.7%	7.1%		92.9%
b)	a	b	c	a	b	c
	7.1%	14.3%	78.6%	50%	50%	0

Conclusion: Women are allowed to gesticulate more expansively than men.

Frame II: Lack of Eye Contact

	female			male		
a)	yes		no	yes		no
	27.6%		72.4%	10.7%		89.3%
b)	a	b	c	a	b	c
	0	0	100%	4.8%	95.2%	0

Conclusion: While these results show that the lack of eye contact is viewed negatively in both cases, it is less acceptable in men. However, there was greater willingness to hire the man without reservations;

Frame III: Aggressiveness

	female			male		
a)	yes		no	yes		no
	55.2%		44.8%	78.6%		21.4%
b)	a	b	c	a	b	c
	12.5%	43.8%	43.8%	9.1%	59%	31.8%

Conclusion: Aggressiveness is viewed more negatively in women than in men.

Frame IV: Fidgeting

	female			male		
a)	yes		no	yes		no
	31%		69%	17.9%		82.1%
b)	a	b	c	a	b	c
	0	11.1%	88.9%	0	20%	80%

Conclusion: Display of nervousness and use of self-adaptors is less acceptable for men than for women.

Frame V: Moderately aggressive

	female			male		
a)	yes	no		yes		no
	100%	0		17.9%		82.1%
b)	a	b	c	a	b	c
	42.9%	50%	7.1%	9.5%	41.6%	42.8%

Conclusion: Indeterminable due to uncontrollable factors.

Question 2: The applicant's intellectual capacity is a) outstanding b) average c) below average

Frame I: Overgesticulation

	female			male	
a	b	c	a	b	c
69%	31%	0	17.9%	71.4%	10.7%

Conclusion: Although verbal response was identical, the woman was judged to be outstanding while the man was found average. Perhaps, people do not expect such an intelligent remark from a woman and thus the strength of the verbal component was overwhelming (see chapter 9).

Frame II: Lack of Eye Contact

	female			male	
a	b	c	a	b	c
31%	65.5%	3.5%	14.3%	71.4%	14.3%

Conclusion: Woman judged more intelligent.

Frame III: Aggressiveness

	female			male	
a	b	c	a	b	c
51.7%	48.3%	0	42.9%	50%	7.1%

Conclusion: Woman judged more intelligent.

Frame IV: Fidgeting

	female			male	
a	b	c	a	b	c
24.1%	75.9%	0	10.7%	75%	14.3%

Conclusion: Woman judged more intelligent.

Frame V: Moderate aggressiveness

	female			male	
a	b	c	a	b	c
69%	31%	0	25%	67.9%	7.1%

Conclusion: Woman judged more intelligent.

Question 3: The applicant appears a) self-reliant b) insecure c) overbearing

Frame I: Overgesticulation

	female			male	
a	b	c	a	b	c
27.6%	0	72.4%	21.4%	0	78.6%

No significant difference.

Frame II: Lack of Eye Contact

	female			male	
a	b	c	a	b	c
0	100%	0	*	*	*

*Male data did not have a total of 28 responses; therefore, no percentages could be included.

Frame III: Aggressiveness

	female			male	
a	b	c	a	b	c
72.4%	3.4%	24.1%	82.1%	7.1%	10.7%

Conclusion: Male is found to be more overbearing.

Frame IV: Fidgeting

	female			male	
a	b	c	a	b	c
0	100%	0	10.7%	82.1%	10.7%

No significant difference.

Frame V: Moderate aggressiveness

	female			male	
a	b	c	a	b	c
100%	0	0	57.1%	25%	17.9%

Conclusion: The same problem is found here as in the first question, fifth frame.

Question 4: Does the applicant appear emotionally stable? a) yes b) no

Frame I: Overgesticulation

	female		male	
a	b		a	b
75.9%	24.1%		53.6%	46.4%

Conclusion: Woman judged more stable. This finding is surprising because it goes against the stereotype of women being emotionally unstable.

Frame II: Lack of Eye Contact

	female		male	
a	b		a	b
44.8%	55.2%		48.1%	51.9%

No significant difference.

Frame III: Aggressiveness

	female		male	
a	b		a	b
96.6%	3.4%		85.7%	14.3%

Conclusion: Woman found more stable.

Frame IV: Fidgeting

	female		male	
a	b		a	b
41.4%	58.6%		40.7%	59.3%

No significant difference.

Frame V: Moderate aggressiveness

	female		male	
a	b		a	b
100%	0		85.7%	14.3%

Indeterminable

Question 5: Does the applicant appear a) highly competent b) adequately competent c) incompetent

Frame I: Overgesticulation

	female			male	
a	b	c	a	b	c
34.5%	55.2%	10.3%	14.3%	71.4%	14.3%

Conclusion: Woman found to be more highly competent.

Frame II: Lack of Eye Contact

	female			male	
a	b	c	a	b	c
0	82.8%	17.2%	3.6%	60.7%	35.7%

Conclusion: On the whole, woman found more competent.

Frame III: Aggressiveness

	female			male	
a	b	c	a	b	c
27.6%	69%	3.4%	32.1%	60.7%	7.1%

No significant difference.

Frame IV: Fidgeting

	female			male	
a	b	c	a	b	c
62.1%	37.9%	0	25%	67.9%	7.1%

Conclusion: Woman found slightly more competent.

Frame V: Moderate aggressiveness

	female			male	
a	b	c	a	b	c
62.1%	37.9%	0	25%	67.9%	7.1%

Conclusion: Woman found to be more highly competent.

Question 6: I would like to have the applicant as: a) a personal friend b) as an acquaintance c) as my boss d) as my employee e) never have anything to do with him/her.

Frame I: Overgesticulation

		female					male		
a	b	c	d	e	a	b	c	d	e
0	20.7%	0	31.0%	48.3%	0	10.7%	3.6%	7.1%	78.6%

Frame II: Lack of Eye Contact

		female					male		
a	b	c	d	e	a	b	c	d	e
0	55.2%	0	13.8%	48.3%	3.6%	28.6%	3.6%	7.1%	57.1%

Frame III: Aggressiveness

		female					male		
a	b	c	d	e	a	b	c	d	e
6.9%	41.4%	0	34.5%	17.2%	10.7%	14.3%	3.6%	60.7%	10.7%

Frame IV: Fidgeting

	female					male			
a	b	c	d	e	a	b	c	d	e
0	55.2%	0	13.8%	31%	0	35.7%	3.6%	10.7%	50%

Frame V: Moderate aggressiveness

	female*					male			
a	b	c	d	e	a	b	c	d	e
17.9%	3.6%	0	78.6%	0	10.7%	14.3%	7.1%	46.4%	21.4%

*One person answered b/d. This response was not included.

Conclusion for question six: It is interesting to note that the woman was never chosen as a boss.

11.1.4. *Conclusion: Rating of female vs. male candidate*

Differences in the evaluation of the same nonverbal behavior in a man or in a women are almost predictably true to stereotype. Overt aggressiveness is viewed more favorably in men than in women and nervously fidgeting men are more severely criticized than women.

On the whole, the female candidate was judged more leniently than the male candidate. Women are at present at an advantage over men in the hiring situation as many industries in the United States of America are under the pressure of Affirmative Action to fill their quotas of female employees. How much such considerations affect the evaluation of an applicant in a simulated interview situation is hard to assess. If at all, it could have affected judgment at the Nissan Corporation but it is doubtful that it had any impact in the context of the hospital or the library as such institutions already have a large number of female employees.

The results from the test are divergent enough with regard to the evaluation of an identical nonverbal behavior when produced by a woman compared to a man to point to real differences in the interpretation of that very same behavior depending on the sex of the sender.

The female applicant on the testing tape was dressed 'appropriately', i.e. in a conservative business-like fashion with a slight feminine touch. She wore a gray woolen skirt and matching well-cut cardigan over a maroon blouse with its high neck closure adorned by a bow ribbon of the same silken material. As mentioned in chapter 10, there is an abundance of books giving advice on how women should dress for a career interview and the authors of these popular books claim that their advice is based on research albeit they do not specify how the information was gathered. The executives which I consulted, gave great emphasis to clothing as part of the all-important first impression. Their statements were reported in chapter 10, pages 97-98. In that chapter I also described the difference in handshake expectancies for men and women. One aspect needs to be covered here as it directly relates my video research comparing male and female applicants. It refers to Frame II where the candidate does not establish adequate eye contact. I asked a male executive whether he expected the same amount of mutual gaze in an interview with a women as he did with a man and he said that yes, he did. He is, of course, aware of the sexual connotations that eye contact can assume but made it clear that the whole interview situation has to be kept free of flirtation and that it is perfectly possible to establish eye contact across the sexes within strict professionalism. All the hiring officials whom I interviewed, men as well as women, emphasized that attempts at flirtation are judged very unfavorably and rule out employment offers, mainly because such behavior 'makes for trouble' in the working context later on.

Hiring officials, however, do not treat men and women in an identical manner socially but state that this has absolutely no bearing on their evaluation process. They will always get up from their seat for a woman candidate and be more 'polite'. In this connection, I would like to refer back to what I said in chapter 10 concerning the high value all interviewers place on etiquette. They are conscious of representing their company and expect from future employees to project an equally positive image.

11.2. *The evaluation of the female candidate depending on the sex of the rater*

When the responses were divided by the male versus the female judges the following results were obtained:

Ratings of Female Applicant by Male
and Female Judges (all professionals)

Male Totals	N = 15 (professionals)		Age range 30-49	
I	II	III	IV	V
1a) 9yes 6no	4yes 11no	7yes 8no	3yes 12no	15yes
b) 1a 1b 7c	4c	3b 4c	1b 2c	7a 6b 1c*
2) 8a 7b	3a 11b 1c	7a 8b	2a 12b 1c	9a 6b
3) 5a 10b	15b	10a 5c	15b	15a
4) 11yes 4no	9yes 6no	14yes 1no	4yes 11no	15yes
5) 3a 9b 3c	14b 1c	2a 13b	1a 10b 4c	11a 4b
6) 3b 5d 7e	6b 2b 7e	1a 6b 5d 3e	7b 2d 6e	3a 11d**

* one omission of part b
** one person answered b/d. His response was not included.

Female Totals	N = 14 (professionals)		Age range 22-60+	
I	II	III	IV	V
1a) 5yes 9no	4yes 10no	9yes 5no	6yes 8no	14yes
b) 1b 4c	4c	2a 4b 3c	6c	5a 8b 1c
2) 12a 2b	6a 8b	8a 6b	5a 9b	11a 3b
3) 3a 11c	14b	11a 1b 2c	14b	14a
4) 11yes 3no	4yes 10no	14yes	6yes 8no	14yes
5) 7a 7b	10b 4c	6a 7b 1c	1a 13b	7a 7b
6) 3b 4d 7e	10b 2d 2e	1a 6b 5d 2e	9b 2d 3e	2a 1b 11d

Ratings of Female Applicant by Male
and Female Judges (all professionals)

Males (n = 15)   Females (n = 14)

Question 1: Would you hire the applicant? A) yes no B) if yes, a) enthusiastically b) without reservations c) with reservations

Frame I: Overgesticulation

	male			female		
	yes		no	yes		no
a)	60%		40%	35.7%		64.3%
	a	b	c	a	b	c
b)	11.1%	11.1%	77.8%	0%	20%	80%

Conclusion: The women were much more critical than the men of excessive gesticulation.

Frame II: Lack of Eye Contact

	male		female	
a)	yes	no	yes	no
	26.7%	73.3%	28.6%	71.4%
b)	a b c		a b c	
	0% 0% 100%		0% 0% 100%	

Conclusion: Barely any difference

Frame III: Aggressiveness

	male		female	
a)	yes	no	yes	no
	46.7%	53.3%	64.3%	35.7%
b)	a b c		a b c	
	0% 42.9% 57.1%		22.2% 44.4% 33.3%	

Conclusion: The women were much more positive about aggressiveness.

Frame IV: Fidgeting

	male		female	
a)	yes	no	yes	no
	20%	80%	42.9%	57.1%
b)	a b c		a b c	
	0% 33.3% 66.6%		0% 0% 100%	

Conclusion: The men were much more critical of fidgeting than the women.

Frame V: Moderate aggressiveness

	male		female	
a)	yes	no	yes	no
	100%	0%	100%	0%
b)	a b c		a b c	
	50% 42.9% 7.1%*		35.7% 57.1% 7.1%	

*one omission of part b

Conclusion: As said before, the data are not compatible.

Question 2: The applicant's intellectual capacity is a) outstanding b) average c) below average

Frame I: Overgesticulation

	male			female	
a	b	c	a	b	c
53.3%	46.7%	0%	85.7%	14.3%	0%

Conclusion: The women were much more impressed with the intellectual capacity of the applicant.

Frame II: Lack of Eye Contact

	male			female	
a	b	c	a	b	c
20%	73.3%	6.7%	42.9%	57.1%	0%

Conclusion: The women were much more impressed with the intellectual capacity of the applicant.

Frame III: Aggressiveness

	male			female	
a	b	c	a	b	c
46.7%	53.3%	0%	57.1%	42.9%	0%

Conclusion: The women were much more impressed with the intellectual capacity of the applicant.

Frame IV: Fidgeting

	male			female	
a	b	c	a	b	c
13.3%	80%	6.7%	35.7%	64.3%	0%

Conclusion: The women were much more impressed with the intellectual capacity of the applicant.

Frame V: Moderate aggressiveness

	male			female	
a	b	c	a	b	c
60%	40%	0%	78.6%	21.4%	0%

Conclusion: Incompatible data

Question 3: The applicant appears a) self-reliant b) insecure c) overbearing

Frame I: Overgesticulation

	male			female		
a	b	c	a	b	c
33.3%	0%	66.7%	21.4%	0%	78.6%

Conclusion: Women tend to consider overgesticulation more indicative of an overbearing personality than men do.

Frame II: Lack of Eye Contact

a	b	c	a	b	c
0%	100%	0%	0%	100%	0%

Conclusion: The responses are identical.

Frame III: Aggressiveness

a	b	c	a	b	c
66.7%	0%	33.3%	78.6%	7.1%	14.3%

Conclusion: Women seldom interpret aggressiveness as stemming from insecurity.

Frame IV: Fidgeting

a	b	c	a	b	c
0%	100%	0%	0%	100%	0%

Conclusion: The responses are identical.

Frame V: Moderate aggressiveness

a	b	c	a	b	c
100%	0%	0%	100%	0%	0%

Conclusion: Incompatible data

Question 4: Does the applicant appear emotionally stable? a) yes b) no

Frame I: Overgesticulation

a	b	a	b
73.3%	26.7%	78.6%	21.4%

Conclusion: The responses are virtually identical.

Frame II: Lack of Eye Contact

	male			female	
a	b		a	b	
60%	40%		28.6%	71.4%	

Conclusion: Men do not correlate lack of eye contact as severely with emotional stability as women do.

Frame III: Aggressiveness

	male			female	
a	b		a	b	
93.3%	6.7%		100%	0%	

Conclusion: Very little difference among the respondents.

Frame IV: Fidgeting

	male			female	
a	b		a	b	
26.7%	73.3%		42.9%	57.1%	

Conclusion: The results are almost opposite.

Frame V: Moderate aggressiveness

	male			female	
a	b		a	b	
100%	0%		100%	0%	

Conclusion: Incompatible data.

Question 5: Does the applicant appear a) highly competent b) adequately competent c) incompetent

Frame I: Overgesticulation

	male			female	
a	b	c	a	b	c
20%	60%	20%	50%	50%	0%

Conclusion: Women tended to attribute a higher degree of competence.

Frame II: Lack of Eye Contact

	male			female	
a	b	c	a	b	c
0%	93.3%	6.7%	0%	71.4%	28.6%

Conclusion: Lack of mutual gaze, again, is less disturbing to men than to women.

Frame III: Aggressiveness

	male			female	
a	b	c	a	b	c
13.3%	86.7%	0%	42.9%	50%	7.1%

Conclusion: Women associate aggressiveness with a higher degree of professional competence than men do.

Frame IV: Fidgeting

	male			female	
a	b	c	a	b	c
6.7%	66.7%	26.6%	7.1%	92.9%	0%

Conclusion: Fidgeting is less indicative of lack of competence for women than for men.

Frame V: Moderate aggressiveness

	male			female	
a	b	c	a	b	c
73.3%	26.6%	0%	50%	50%	0%

Conclusion: Incompatible data.

Question 6: I would like to have the applicant as: a) a personal friend b) as an acquaintance c) as my boss d) as my employee e) never have anything to do with him/her.

Frame I: Overgesticulation

		male					female		
a	b	c	d	e	a	b	c	d	e
0%	20%	0%	33.3%	46.7%	0%	21.4%	0%	28.6%	50%

Conclusion: True to their dislike of excessive gesticulation, several women did not want any personal association with the candidate while no man went that far.

Frame II: Lack of Eye Contact

		male					female		
a	b	c	d	e	a	b	c	d	e
0%	40%	0%	13.3%	46.7%	0%	71.4%	0%	14.3%	14.3%

Conclusion: On a personal basis, gaze avoidance is far more unattractive to men than to women.

Frame III: Agressiveness

	male					female			
a	b	c	d	e	a	b	c	d	e
6.7%	40%	0%	33.3%	20%	7.1%	42.9%	0%	35.7%	14.3%

Conclusion: The responses are greatly similar.

Frame IV: Fidgeting

	male					female			
a	b	c	d	e	a	b	c	d	e
0%	46.7%	0%	13.3%	40%	0%	64.3%	0%	14.3%	21.4%

Conclusion: In a personal relationship, fidgeting is a more undesirable trait for men than for women.

Frame V: Moderate aggressiveness

	male					female			
a	b	c	d	e	a	b	c	d	e
21.4%	0%	0%	78.6%	0%*	14.3%	7.1%	0%	78.6%	0%

*One person answered b/d. This response was not included.

Conclusion: Incompatible data.

Conclusion: The evaluation of nonverbal behavior depending on the same-sex or other-sex relationship between the subject and the rater

In a female applicant women raters exhibit less tolerance for excessive gesticulation than men do but are less disturbed by nervous fidgeting. Women value aggressiveness in a woman higher than men do but are more negative towards a female candidate who does not establish adequate eye contact. On the overall, when it comes to hiring a female applicant, women are more lenient judges than men. Almost an equal number of men hired or rejected the candidate (total from all frames: 38 yes/37 no). A slightly greater number of women were inclined to hire her (total from all frames: 38 yes/32 no).

When comparing the women's responses to the female applicant with the women's responses to the male applicant, the ratings in many instances are exactly opposite. Furthermore, in many instances the ratio of male and female response to a same-sex or other-sex candidate was reversed. Such a reversal was particularly evident with regard to Frame II (lack of eye contact). Although male hiring officials had told me that they expect the same amount of mutual gaze during an interview with a woman and with a man applicant, in actuality, male raters were far less negative about a woman who lacked eye contact than about a man. Women were far more tolerant of nervous fidgeting in a female applicant than in a male. An example of consistency in same-sex and other-sex relationship is the liking women have for aggressive candidates.

The results of this cursory comparison of the responses of male and female raters to the nonverbal behavior of men and women point to the dire need for further research into the differences among men and women in the perception of nonverbal behavior but even more so into the differences in the performance evaluation of same-sex and other-sex subjects. My research is meant to be a beginning and not a final conclusion. Research is needed involving a large number of same-sex and other-sex senders to be judged by an even larger number of raters.

This is an area which can only be researched with the multiple design approach. If the same subject population rates the male and the female applicant, they may be swayed by the contrast effect (Hakel *et al.* 1970a). If different raters are used for the two sexes, a very large number of subjects is needed to make certain that sex-related differences are not accidental. It is therefore best to split the raters and have some evaluate both male and female candidates, and also alternating the sequence of the presentation of the two videotapes. In any case, it is essential to present tapes of a considerable number of male and of female candidates to avoid that the likeability of a candidate might be the determining factor influencing judgment. Besides performance evaluation forms like the one I have used throughout on structured tests, I would suggest that more hiring officials be interviewed informally. The latter procedure has provided many valuable insights. It may be beyond anybody's time disposibility to match the male and female judges for age and years of experience, not to mention sameness of position within the corporate structure.

Since Webster (1964) wrote his classic on the career interview almost twenty years ago, much remains still to be done in this field in regard to nonverbal behavior.

12. THE MINORITY APPLICANT

The federal government distinguishes between four categories of *protected groups*, the aged, minorities, women, and the handicapped. There are seven federal agencies watching over compliance and the regulations are sometimes conflicting. The *Kiplinger Newsletter* keeps industry abreast of new and up-coming legislation. Large companies have to meet quotas but small businesses are not obligated to actively recruit women and minorities. There is no obligation to recruit among the elderly. A corporation is investigated for discrimination only when there is a blatant charge but the law favors the protected groups because they are the only parties that can file suit, and the media tend to give ample coverage to discrimination suits. Interviewers are not permitted to ascertain whether an applicant belongs to a protected group. Information about at least some of these factors is generally available from the applicant's resumé. As I mentioned earlier, I thought that sex was always apparent during an interview but was proven wrong when one employer told me that he interviewed a person dressed like a woman who then the next day on the job turned out to be a man in regular man's attire. It would have been illegal for the employer to object to the fact that he thought that he had hired a woman when in reality he had hired a man.

Although the U.S. government regulations forbid asking any questions even indirectly relating to age, sex, race, or national origin, Washington is greatly concerned with affirmative action towards its minorities. Members of a minority are considered those who have at least one grandparent who fits any of the following categories: an American Indian; an Alaskan native; a person of Chinese, Japanese, Korean, or Filipino origin; a person of Mexican, Puerto Rican, or Cuban extraction or originally of Spanish culture; a person having some ancestor of black African descent. Thus a minority is defined by the law as one who the law considers non-white. There are seven federal agencies to comply with and it is extremely complicated because the regulations are sometimes conflicting.

In business jargon the racial make-up for legal purposes is called COINS: Caucasian, Oriental, Indian, Negro and Spanish surnamed.

12.1. *Employers' attitudes*

Potential employers are extremely conscious of race as they operate under the constant threat of legal discrimination suits. In case of suits, even if an employer is able to prove that his hiring evaluation was not discriminatory, the cost of defending himself in court can be onerous (Morgan 1980: 2).

Some executives suggest that government regulations really work against minorities because they make it next to impossible to consider a minority person like everybody else and to dismiss him if he does not work out. If there are various applicants who have sent in their resumés and among them is a competent minority person, it is risky to invite him for an interview because in case he turns out not to be the best of the ones invited for an interview, it becomes extremely cumbersome to document why he was not chosen. So it is safer to find an initial justification for not asking him for an interview to begin with. Corporate officials in firms which practice the exit interview told me that they spend far more time with a minority member than with any other employee that resigned or had to be terminated. They do this not only for their own legal protection but primarily because more than ever they want to find out what caused the deficiency on the job. They watch for 'signs of nervousness' more intensely than during exit interviews with non-minority employees. 'Signs of nervousness' are said to manifest themselves "through the voice and through the body". Personnel officers feel that the hiring of minorities required more time and energy than working with non-minorities and unconsciously they may shy away from this.

Contrary to those that believe that the legal obligations, in the final analysis, work against minorities, others believe that the government greatly helps minorities, and black people in particular, because without pressure, prejudice would prevail excluding them from many job opportunities.

It is well known that job discrimination may occur beyond the categories officially designated as vulnerable. My research, nevertheless, is limited to the official categories and what I have investigated is how the nonverbal behavior of members of these groups during the career interview is evaluated by potential employers. The career interview which has been the focus of my research concerns lower and middle management and candidates have at least a bachelor's degree. Generalizations cannot be drawn for unskilled work, labor, or office help. The dissertation by Chavez Fernandez (1980) has many features that are compatible with my research design but her black subjects are totally incompatible with mine in socio-educational background as well as job aspirations.

De la Zerda's (1980: 77-78) dissertation examines the impact of ethnic speech markers in the employment interview. Her results show that a Mexican-American accent affects hiring decision in increasing order in direct correlation with the increase in the level of the position for which an applicant is considered. Generalizations across social classes and job specifications cannot be drawn with regard to minority interviewing either for the verbal or the nonverbal factors.

In this chapter I will report on the information I gained about minorities during the meetings with business officials which I described in chapter 9. Most of my corporate respondents were white males, one third of whom belonged in the protected age group. One fourth of my respondents were women, two thirds over forty years old. Only one respondent belonged to a racially defined minority. He was a black male in his late thirties. Concerning the counselors of the six employment agencies whom I canvassed, half of them belonged to the protected age group, two were men and four were women; none had a minority background. I have also talked with two presidents of job training centers, one a white woman, the other a black man, and with two white male deans of a graduate business school.

I have searched the literature on how to conduct job interviews which is used by personnel officers, in the form of commercially printed brochures, as well as in-house publications. A computer search for studies on minorities in the job interview revealed only one item dealing with physical appearance and nonverbal behavior (Chavez Fernandez 1980) and absolutely nothing on minority interviews for upper level positions.

I have not researched the hiring process of handicapped persons. The literature on their behalf is ample and would have required an enormous amount of time to survey. Informal sessions with people that were physically disabled revealed that they feel strongly discriminated against. The handicapped who cannot hide their disabilities see their only hope in strong government intervention.

One thing is certain: Every interviewer looks at the candidate's physical traits and classifies him in one of the COINS categories before starting the questioning period. As said above, small companies have no set quota and therefore are not obligated to actively recruit minorities. Some companies avoid hiring minorities, either out of their own prejudices or because they believe that it would hurt their image with potential customers. Employment agencies find out whether minorites are welcome before they send them on to companies. There are also differences in the treatment of the various types of minorities. Black persons are generally the last ones to be hired voluntarily, but also the ones most sought after to comply with government pressure. Orientals rank on the other extreme. They are well-liked because they are considered hard working, intelligent, and easy to get along with.

Eiko Taguchi, a graduate student of mine who is Japanese, rated the Five

Frames videotape described in chapter 10, page 85, and also showed it to three other graduate students from Japan. These judges were 24, 31, 32, and 34 years old. Except for Ms. Taguchi who is female and specializing in linguistics, all others were males and seeking advanced degrees in economics or engineering. They held jobs in Japan to which they planned to return. One had been working as a personnel officer for four years between 1976 and 1980. Their performance evaluation is remarkably similar to that of the American professionals. Nobody would hire the applicant who failed to have eye contact nor the one who fidgeted. The female rater and the youngest of the male raters would hire the overgesticulator 'with reservations' and select him 'as an acquaintance'. One other male rater would also hire him 'with reservations' but 'never have anything to do with him'. The two remaining raters, including the man with four years of personnel experience, would not hire him but like him 'as an acquaintance'. The moderately aggressive applicant on Frame V who behaved in his own natural manner received the highest ratings throughout and was the only one who was wanted 'as a personal friend'. The one who did not select him as a friend still liked to have him 'as an acquaintance'.

None of these foreign students had been in the United States for more than two years and all their social life centered within the Japanese community. It is truly remarkable how accurately they interpreted the five frame variations in terms of employability. When I spoke about this with some Japanese friends of mine, they told me that they work hard and efficiently at studying another culture when they enter into relations with it. Maybe this is the reason why Asians are believed to be 'easy to work with'. They make a concerted effort at understanding the other culture, at what I might call 'surface accomodation'.

Mr. Bud Curtis, who is an executive of a national insurance firm, told me that insurance agencies like to hire people from different races to match their prospective clients. An interesting approach is practiced by a large American discount chain, Service Merchandise. This firm tries to represent within each of their affiliates on a percentage basis the racial make-up of each city in which they operate. They believe that their work force should match their clientele. In a similar vein, some American department stores blend their sales personnel with the section of town which they serve. Then there are instances where race is part of the job desiderata, if not requirements. Chinese restaurants or Mexican gift shops prefer their representatives to 'play the part'. Foreign students are sought after as waiters and waitresses by fancy restaurants. Any foreign accent is supposed to sound French. Fast-food chains near college campuses like to give an air of cosmopolitan mix. The 40-65 age group is favored among saleswomen catering to the not-so-young, such as buyers of oversized foundations.

Once the race of a candidate is established the interviewer looks for exactly the same qualifications he would look for in a Caucasian applicant. Interviewers from large national companies are knowledgeable about racial and cultural differences in nonverbal behavior having learned these in their training sessions or follow-up workshops. Interviewers from smaller companies that are not cognizant of the exact differences nevertheless make automatic adjustments. If, for example, they find differences in the pattern of eye contact between black and white candidates they do not worry over this. They simply judge whether eye contact was maintained in whatever form. Interviewers also spend more time with persons of races with which they are less familiar realizing that people have greater difficulty in understanding facial and body expressions that are divergent from their own. One guidebook (Calbert 1972, quoted in Pell (1980: 12)) explicitly cautions, "Don't let minor things bother you ... For example, wearing dark glasses represents a symbol of affluence and status in certain milieus."

These are adjustments most interviewers make voluntarily and find quite reasonable. Other adjustments are made reluctantly and only because they are forced on them by law. Most disliked in minorities during the past decade were large Afros, but they were really disliked not more intensely than the long hairstyles of white youths fashionable some years earlier. Grooming is always essential. Nowadays employers only insist that hair be well kept and in style. Legally this is a grey area. The law explicitly forbids to have hairstyle requirements that are racially discriminatory. In general, U.S. law does not require differential rating scales for mainstream and minority candidates with regard to nonverbal behavior. To insure that written tests are used fairly, the EEOC Guidelines (Equal Opportunity Commission 1970) and the APA Standards (American Psychological Association 1974) require differential validation studies whenever "technically feasible" (Ford 1980: 2). Nothing of this sort has been formulated for the judgment of nonverbal forms of expression.

Charles Storey, a regional director of INROAD and a black man himself, believes that our society is not yet ready for cultural diversity. He trains minority students interested in a business career to behave like white junior executives. He advises them to hold their hands together if they tend to overgesticulate, to sit with their legs crossed, and to walk without the sense of rhythm that is characteristic of black peoples. He even teaches them to use the larger hand movements of the white man and to avoid the small baton movements that are common in black conversation. His students are told to wear conservative suits and no jewelry. It is very hard for young people to learn a foreign body rhythm but Mr. Storey believes that conformity in language, body movements, and general appearance is the only avenue to success in the business world. The track record of his students seem to prove him right. According to the personnel executives whom I have interviewed, absolute conformity is not a prerequisite but a certain amount of it is essential (von Raffler-Engel 1981).

A study is warranted on the degree and type of ethnic peculiarities which are acceptable in business. There appears to be a discrepancy between what employers are willing to accept, or say they are willing to accept, and what minorities perceive as acceptable.

As the job market opens up for those that have been previously excluded, it remains to be seen whether all the newcomers will conform to the establishment or whether they will cause general changes in the appearance and in the mode of behavior of the total population. To give an example, will women continue wearing tailored suits and carry briefcases, or is this only a transitional stage? (von Raffler-Engel 1980e).

What I have reported in this chapter is what corporate interviewers have told me. I have no reason to assume that they purposely hid any information from me nor that they generally do not act in good faith, either in their interviewing practices or in their criteria for selection of minority candidates. In a general way, they seem aware of the pitfalls of the similar-to-me effect (see chapter 7) when they state that it takes somewhat longer to examine a person from a culture divergent from their own. I doubt, however, that many of them realize the subconsicous difficulties in cross-cultural communication (von Raffler-Engel 1980d). Black officials were an exception to this as they immediately grasped what I was talking about when I spoke of body rhythm and the need for conversational interactants to adjust to each other, which in effect amounts to the less dominant one adjusting to the other. For future research it is desirable to supplement my questionnaire establishing the hierarchy of nonverbal behaviors with a systematic survey of employers' attitudes in a more generalized fashion.

12.2. *How the minority candidate perceives himself*

During the last three years I have held informal conversations with members of diverse minorities in the United States of America in regard to how they feel about their body motions when they go to be interviewed for a position. All realize that they are expected to conform to mainstream characteristics. While prospects for jobs were good, some felt that they could keep their traditional behavior, implying that a prospective employer could 'take them as they were' or leave them. With the shrinking labor market, this option is no longer viable. In respect to how they feel about mainstreaming minorities fall into two distinct categories. Members of one category, composed largely of Orientals, feel that they have a strong identity which is totally unaffected by the way they behave outside their own community. On the other extreme are Black Americans that feel that they had to 'give in' for so many generations that to do this now that they finally regained their 'pride' is a very high price to pay even for the chance of earning a livelihood.

American Indians are divided over the issue and Indian tribes should never be lumped together in any generalized statement. According to Mr. Jerry Webster, project director for Community Development of the Southern and Eastern Tribes which include the Malisletse, the two factions of the Passama-quoddy tribe and the Penobscot Nation, all in Maine; the St. Regis Mohawk tribe and Seneca Nation of New York; the Eastern Band of Cherokees in North Carolina; the Mississippi Band of Choctaws; the Chitimacha and Choushatta tribes in Louisiana, and the Seminole and Miccosukee tribes of Florida, presently there are very few Indians who aspire to positions in corporate management. Most Indians are traditionally oriented and want to live on their reservations. Of the non-reservation Indians most prefer the rural life style to the urban one and keep a communal rural life pattern even when they are city dwellers. The few Indians who go to college and even those who get the MBA degree find it extremely difficult to adjust to the competitive life style of the business world. They are group-oriented rather than striving towards lone, individual achievement. During the interview they feel deferent towards the authority status of the interviewer, and particularly so if he is an older man. Courtesy demands that they not be muscle-tense but relaxed when sitting in front of him. It is cultur-ally very difficult for Indians to establish constant eye contact or lean for-ward aggressively. Generally, they have a positive self-image and a firm hand-shake but fail to project the image of a 'go-getter'. They have no moral objec-tions to people who are success-oriented but, with few exceptions, do not feel it worth their while to radically change their philosophy of life for the sake of financial gain. They do not wish to alter a sedate body rhythm into a dynamic one. The result of this is usually a negative assessment in the employment inter-view.

Given the limits of time and manpower I have restricted my small-scale indepth research project to Black Americans which form the ethnic group most familiar to me and which also is the largest one in the United States. An attempt to show a Five Frames videotape with a black candidate analogous to the one used for the male and female white applicants (see chapters 10 and 11) failed due to technical difficulties.

One of my Black students, Chandra Taylor, contacted some of the black students she knew in Nashville, Tennessee, and asked them to describe how they behaved, or planned to behave, in a career interview with a white official. The students compiled the usual personal data sheet (see Appendix II). Their experience in having been previously interviewed amounted to two on the average. These undergraduates were enrolled at Vanderbilt University (VU), a predominantly white upper middle class university and at Tennessee State University (TSU), a predominantly black lower middle class university. The total number of subjects was 9 and they formed the following factorial design:

4M		5F		5VU			4TSU
2VU	2TSU	4VU	1TSU	2M	3F	3M	1F

All respondents mentioned that they will present themselves 'with decorum', jacket and tie for men, conservative dress for women. The woman from the black institution also made sure that her nail polish was in perfect order. All respondents said that they will 'slow down their speech' so that they will be sure to enunciate clearly and, above all, to have time to formulate their thoughts coherently. All said that they will 'hold back their gesticulation'.

The university attended by the students caused no differences in kind but some in degree. Students attending Black institutions spend more time and emphasis on mentioning the clarity of speech. They also seem to be more nervous about the whole situation and feel that they have to 'work hard' at it, while students at Vanderbilt University say that they will behave like they do with their white professors and by the time they are seniors they have "met quite a lot of them".

The real division on the responses runs along the sex line. Women, on the whole, are less apprehensive about the situation and do not mention 'caution'. With regard to specific behaviors, they will be careful not to cross their legs in a way that would expose their thighs but keep them close together in parallel or cross them at the ankle. Women will establish firm and consistent eye contact, "look the interviewer straight in the eye". Three of the Vanderbilt women intend to give the impression of a 'pensive look', one by tilting her head slightly to the side, two by putting their hand to the chin. All women will give 'a firm handshake'. One Vanderbilt woman said that she will have to make a real effort to come across as aggressive because, really, she is "not at all an aggressive type". She will also sit straight up and hold her hands together so as "not to use her hands nervously". In conclusion, it appears that the women are primarily concerned to come across business-like and not to show signs of weakness that could be interpreted as traditionally feminine behavior. For whatever reason, either because they had some assertiveness training for women or other, black females seem more aware of their status as women than as blacks.

The men appear more conscious of being black, or rather, for them, being male and black are two attributes that cannot be separated. They feel that their pride demands that they "will not behave like a white". They "want to be the best as a black person" and "to use their own movements effectively" so as not "to squelch their identity". They recognize, however, that 'caution' is demanded of them if they want to succeed in mainstream society. They will establish eye contact but not forcefully and not for too long a period at one time. These men know that there are still many white people who would prefer that they never gain positions of power and do not want to meet them as equals in the face-to-face interaction. The curtailment in time and frequency of mutual gaze was particularly pronounced on the part of men who happen to have particularly deep voices. All men distinguish between assertiveness and aggressiveness. Most white job seekers make that same distinction but are far less worried about coming across as over-agressive. It has to be noted, however, that one black student whose career goal is to become the founder and president of his own consulting firm, was not worried about the optimal degree of aggressiveness but intended to be as aggressive as he can. Whether this depends on the fact that he has higher aspirations, a more slender body build, or more confidence in the labor market because of his degree in one of the few expanding fields, cannot be ascertained.

In conclusion, when a minority person does not switch kinesic code when interacting with the majority, he attenuates his in-group body movements. As shown in my previous research on inter-group kinesics, in situations of an uneven power relationship there are three forms of kinesics, the two normal codes and the reduced code of the social minority (von Raffler-Engel 1976a, 1976b, 1983).

13. THE USE OF NONVERBAL CUES IN
DETERMINING SKILL QUALIFICATIONS

Up to now, this book has dealt with the impact a job applicant's nonverbal behavior has on the hiring decision. It has looked primarily into how nonverbal behavior affects the appraisal of an individual's personality and general suitability for joining the firm represented by the perceiver. The qualifications for the work per se were assumed to be determined from an applicant's resumé the approval of which was a necessary condition of granting him the interview to begin with. Evaluations of nonverbal behavior in relation to the work to be performed were considered only in broad terms. Two general areas were considered. One was whether the candidate was to have contact with the public or not. Judgment in this area focused primarily on manifestations of nervousness, such as fidgeting and use of self-manipulators. The second area distinguished between sales and non-sales jobs. Decisions on the hiring of salesmen were influenced by the candidates' 'forcefulness', as manifested by emphatic gesticulation.

During the career interview nonverbal behavior plays a vital role but it is by no means the sole criterion for judgment. The content of what a candidate says and how well he expresses himself verbally are of vital importance. His paralanguage also greatly influences the rating. There is one type of evaluation, however, which is based on nonverbal behavior exclusively, the Action Profile.

The Action Profile. During the years of prosperity and frequent expansions, firms liked to hire young people of great promise just to make certain that they would not join the competition. In the present hard economic times and frequent retrenchments this happens only in the rarest of cases. What happens more frequently is that personnel is recycled to new departments when their original place of work becomes obsolete and they are too valuable or too well connected to simply let go. In such instances, a determination has to be made on where the individual would best fit. This also applies when promotion from within is contemplated.

There is still another area where changes in the allocation of duties are demanded of an employee. As I said in the Introduction, increasing emphasis is put on team work. In organizing an effective team it is important that the members of the group are compatible and that their competencies complement each other rather than overlap.

The assignation of new duties and/or the composition of team membership is based on the 'fit' of the individual to the task. One way to determine the optimum match between personality and task is by examining an individual's Action Profile.

This procedure was pioneered and subsequently improved by a British industrial consultant, Warren Lamb (Lamb and Turner 1969), and an Australian psychologist, Pamela Ramsden (Ramsden 1973). As summarized by Peters (1973: 48), "The basic idea is that each individual spontaneously selects a combination of postures and gestures which reflect his 'built-in and relatively constant motivational states'." Lamb and Ramsden analyze only the totality of 'posture-gesture mergings'. They do not take into consideration isolated hand gesticulation and facial expression as these are overwhelmingly connected with the content of what is said. Only the integrated patterning of the movements of the trunk, the head, and the arms are believed to be indicative of an individual's inherent emotional patterning. According to the authors, there are three basic types of 'self-motivating states'. Some people are primarily 'communicators' while others are 'presenters' or 'operators'.

Communicators like to investigate and to explore a problem. They are born researchers. Their movements look like a golf club swing, indirecting and directing. Presentors look like newscasters on television, with stylized up and down movements that spread and enclose. They make excellent public relations people. Operators are bouncy, advancing and retreating their torso with shaping movements of their arms and hands. They are destined to be managers, the people that get things implemented. The chart on the opposite page from Peters (1973: 47) will clarify the function of each type of individual within corporate decision making process.

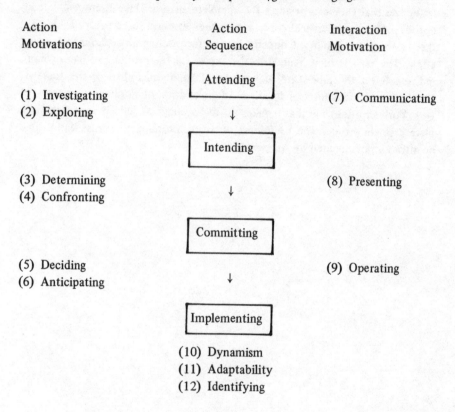

FRAMEWORK OF MANAGEMENT ACTION
FOR
ACTION PROFILING FOR TOP TEAM PLANNING
Effort/shape analysis of posture/gesture mergings

Action Motivations	Action Sequence	Interaction Motivation
	Attending	
(1) Investigating		(7) Communicating
(2) Exploring	↓	
	Intending	
(3) Determining		(8) Presenting
(4) Confronting	↓	
	Committing	
(5) Deciding		(9) Operating
(6) Anticipating	↓	
	Implementing	
	(10) Dynamism	
	(11) Adaptability	
	(12) Identifying	

Of course, nobody is 100% of one type only. It is the duty of the analyst to determine the percentage of an indivual's motivational state. This is accomplished by classifying the direction, intensity, frequency, and variation of the person's movements that make up his 'effort/shape' into the following twelve categories of human attitudes of which these movements are indicative: (1) investigating, (2) exploring, (3) determining, (4) confronting, (5) deciding, (6) anticipating, (7) communicating, (8) presenting, (9) operating, (10) dynamism, (11) adaptability, and (12) identifying.

The 'profiling' is done by professional kinecisists trained in the Ramsden method. Originally, the expert would sit down for up to two hours of video recording with the individual to be profiled and then, in most instances, send the tape for analysis to Ramsden. Nowadays more experts have been adequately trained so that they can perform the complete analysis. Like Ramsden, he may not even have any personal contact with the person(s) to be profiled. Usually, the videotape is produced directly by the firm during a two hour long social affair. The tape is then handed to the expert for the profiling of one or more individuals on the tape. One such expert, Prof. Lynn Cohen of the Josef A. Martino Graduate School of Business Administration of Fordham University in New York City tells me that it takes up to two days of full-time work to complete a single profile. The usefulness of action profiling to industries in three countries is documented by Arbose (1979).

CONCLUSION

There are three approaches to nonverbal behavior when an individual is matched to a task.

One is the assessment of that individual's inherent motivational state whether he is drawn to research, exposition, or managing. This is done through the Action Profile.

The second is the rating of a person's energy and drive. This is done by watching for signs of forcefulness and aggressiveness, such as eye contact and appropriate gesticulation.

The third is the evaluation of the individual's willingness to get along with people. His cooperativeness is judged by his ability for establishing rapport through posture echoing.

In conclusion, an individual's nonverbal behavior is considered a significant indicator of his suitability for performing a previously defined task. The appropriateness of a certain type of nonverbal behavior is gauged within set parameters of intensity. The differences of the effect of the intensity of nonverbal behavior are not significant within the high and low extremes outside the optimal range as is evident from the results of the study by Sterrett (1978). My findings suggest that a nonverbal behavior is considered either within the range of appropriateness or outside of it. In addition, the background of the rater influences his judgment and so does the sex of the person being evaluated.

If prospective employers did not attribute vital importance to nonverbal behavior, they would not invest time and money to personally examine job applicants. They would rely on verifying their resumés and checking the references. If oral expression were the only criterion for selection, the interview might as well be conducted over the telephone. Chavez Fernandez (1980: 2) reports that "in a survey of Metropolitan Kansan City employers, 100% (n. 39) replied that the personal interview was of great importance" The performance of applicants during the interview was also said to be the sole reason for many rejections. In that survey, 79% of the interviewers rated appearance items as 'essential' and 81% classified eye contact and correct posture as 'essential' for the approval of a candidate (Chavez Fernandez 1980: 4).

Any disagreement with the basic assumption that nonverbal behavior is not significant (Sterrett 1978) is likely due to research designs that are not applicable to the fundamental issue treated in this book.

APPENDIX I
Personal Data

Name (optional) . . . .
Company (optional) . . . .

PERSONAL DATA

Sex M F (circle)   Age 24-25 26-29 30-33 34-39 40-43 44-49
50-60 60+ (circle)

Profession: Professor . . . . Years of experience in
Professional Person . . . . personnel . . . .
Undergraduate Student . . . . . .
Graduate Student . . . .
Area of Concentration . . . .
Are you currently: working part-time . . . .
working full-time . . . .
job title . . . .
What are your career goals . . . .

Have you ever been interviewed (circle)
1) for a part-time or summer job? never 2-5 times
once 6-10 times
more than 10 times
2) for a regular, full-time job? never 2-5 times
once 6-10 times
more than 10 times

Have you ever interviewed job applicants (circle)
1) for a part-time or summer job: never 2-5 times
once 6-10 times
more than 10 times
2) for a regular, full-time job? never 2-5 times
once 6-10 times
more than 10 times

Please provide below any further information you believe might be useful to us in assessing your knowledge of the interview situation. Please indicate whether you are or have been working in a personnel department or an employment agency.

APPENDIX II

Performance Ratings

Answer all the questions (1-6) from top to bottom on each column. Each column corresponds to a segment on the videotape.

1. a) Would you hire the applicant? Yes No b) If yes, would you hire the applicant a) enthusiastically c) without reservations c) with reservations

2. The applicant's intellectual capacity is a) outstanding b) average c) below average

3. The applicant appears: a) self-reliant b) insecure c) overbearing

4. Does the applicant appear emotionally stable? Yes No

5. Does the applicant appear: a) highly competent b) adequately competent c) incompetent

6. Outside of any professional consideration I would like to have the applicant as: a) a personal friend b) an acquaintance c) my boss d) my employee e) never have anything to do with him.

ANSWERS

1) I.a. . . . . . II.a. . . . . III.a. . . . IV.a. . . . V.a. . . . . VI.a. . . . . .
    b. . . . .   b. . . . .   b. . . .   b. . . .   b. . . . .   b. . . . . .

2) I. . . . . . II. . . . . . III. . . . . IV. . . . . V. . . . . . VI. . . . . . .

3) I. . . . . . II. . . . . . III. . . . . IV. . . . . V. . . . . . VI. . . . . . .

4) I. . . . . . II. . . . . . III. . . . . IV. . . . . V. . . . . . VI. . . . . . .

5) I. . . . . . II. . . . . . III. . . . . IV. . . . . V. . . . . . VI. . . . . . .

6) I. . . . . . II. . . . . . III. . . . . IV. . . . . V. . . . . . VI. . . . . . .

REFERENCES

Arbose, Jules
1979   "Movements reveal corporate misfits". International Management 34:3.22-25.

Argyle, Michael and Mark Cook
1976   Gaze and mutual gaze. Cambridge: Cambridge University Press.

Bochner, Stephen
1982   "The social psychology of cross-cultural relations". In S. Bochner (ed.), Cultures in contact. Oxford: Pergamon Press, 5-44.

Bok, Derek C.
1981   "The president's report". Harvard Magazine 83:June.23-35.

Boyle, Kammer, Cynthia Thompson, Erick Sundstrom, and Robert Dipboye
1980   Judged competence of job interviewees: Nonverbal behaviors, perceived personality, and sex. Knoxville, Tennessee: University of Tennessee. Unpublished manuscript.

Buck, Ross
1975   "Nonverbal communication of affect in preschool children". Journal of Personality and Social Psychology 32.644-653.

Calvert, Robert, Jr.
1972   Equal employment opportunity for minority group college graduates. Garrett Park, MD: Garrett Park Press.

Campbell, D.T. and D.W. Fiske
1959   "Convergent and discriminant validation by the multitrait-multimethod matrix". Psychological Bulletin 56.81-105.

Chavez Fernandez, Arminda Leonor
1980   The experimental analysis and training of employment interview skills with minority adults. Ann Arbor, Michigan: University Microfilms International 77-16, 266. (Ph.D. dissertation, University of Kansas, 1976.)

De la Zerda, Nancy Jane
1980   Employment interviewers' reaction to Mexican American speech. Ann Arbor, Michigan: University Microfilms International 77-29, 016. (Ph.D. dissertation, University of Texas at Austin, 1977.)

Dipboye, Robert L., Howard L. Fromkin, and Kent Wiback
1975   "Relative importance of applicant sex, attractiveness, and scholastic standing in evaluation of job applicants' resumés". Journal of Applied Psychology 60:1.39-43.

Dipboye, Robert L., Richard D. Arvey, and David E. Terpstra
1977   "Sex and physical attractiveness of raters and applicants as determinants of resumé evaluations". Journal of Applied Psychology 62.288-294.

Edmondson, Willis
1981   Spoken discourse: A model for analysis. London: Longman.

Ekman, Paul
1980   "Three classes of nonverbal behavior". In W. von Raffler-Engel (ed.), 89-102.

Evans, Franklin B.
1963   "Selling as a dyadic relationship – A new approach". American Behavioral Scientist 6.76-79.

Fear, Richard A.
1978   The evaluation interview, 2nd revised edition. New York: McGraw-Hill.

Firestone, Marsha
1982   "Applications: Managerial competence and interaction assessment". Kinesis Report 4:2.10-13.

Ford, Kenneth Arthur
1980   Ethnic group differences in employment tests – Job performance relationships. Ann Arbor, Michigan: University Microfilms International 77-24, 829. (Ph. D. dissertation, University of Southern California, 1976.)

French, Patrice
1973   "Kinesics in communication: Black and white!". The Language Sciences 28.13-16.

1980   "An experimental methodology for kinesic research". In W. von Raffler-Engel (ed.), 173-176.

Golightly, C., D.M. Huffman, and D. Byrne
1972   "Liking and loaning". Journal of Applied Psychology 56.521-523.

Hakel, Milton D., James P. Ohnesorg, and Marvin D. Dunnette
1970a   "Relative importance of three content dimensions in overall suitability rating of job applicants' resumés". Journal of Applied Psychology 54:1.65-71.

1970b   "Interviewer evaluation of job applicants' resumés as a function of the qualifications of the immediately preceding applicants: An examination of contrast effects". Journal of Applied Psychology 54:1.27-30.

Hall, Judith A.
1978   "Gender effects in decoding nonverbal cues". Psychological Bulletin 85:4. 854-857.

Hulbert, James and Noel Capon
1972   "Interpersonal communication in marketing: An overview". Journal of Marketing Research 9.27-34.

Jones, Judson P. and Walburga von Raffler-Engel
1982   "Transactions at a store counter". In M. Davis (ed.), Interaction rhythms. New York: Human Sciences Press, 341-349. (Proceedings of the Annual Re-

search Conference of the Institute for Nonverbal Communications Research. New York, Teachers College, Columbia University, 1979.)

Lamb, Warren and David Turner
1969 Management behavior. London: Duckworth.

London, Manuel and Milton D. Hakel
1974 "Effects of applicant stereotypes, order, and information on interview impressions". Journal of Applied Psychology 59:2.157-162.

London, Manuel and John R. Poplawski
1976 "Effects of information on stereotype development in performance appraisal and interview contexts". Journal of Applied Psychology 61.199-205.

Lykken, D.T.
1968 "Statistical significance in psychological research". Psychological Bulletin 70.151-159.

McGovern, Thomas and Harry Ideus
1978 "The impact of nonverbal behavior on the employment interview". Journal of College Placement Spring. 51-53.

Mehrabian, Albert
1968 "Communication without words". Psychology Today 24.52-55.

Moine, Donald
1982 "To trust, perchance to buy". Psychology Today 16.50-54.

Morgan, Henry H. and John W. Cogger
1980 The interviewer's manual, 2nd edition. New York: Drake-Beam Associates.

Morris, Desmond
1977 Manwatching: A field guide to human behavior. New York: Harry N. Abrams.

Nahemow, Lucille and M. Powell Lawton.
1975 "Similarity propinquity in friendship formation". Journal of Personality and Social Psychology 32:2.205-213.

Pell, Arthur R.
1980 Be a better interviewer: A guide for the screening interview. Huntington, NY: Personnel Publications.

Peters, Alan
1973 "Hoover spring-cleans an executive suite". Business Administration September. 47-49.

Ramsden, Pamela
1973 Top team planning: A study of the power of individual motivaton in management. London: Associated Business Programmes, and New York: Wiley & Sons.

Rand, Thomas M. and Kenneth N. Wexley
1976 Demonstration of the effect 'similar to me' in simulated employment interviews. PPG Industries Applied Behavior Research, Pittsburgh, PA Pamphlet.

Snyder, Mark
  1980   "The many me's of the self-monitor". Psychology Today 92.30-40.

Soxology
  1970   Family Weekly, the Newspaper Magazine. June 14.

Sterrett, John H.
  1976   "A study of the relationship between nonverbal communication and percep-
          tions of qualities associated with effectiveness in the insurance industry".
          Dissertation Abstracts International 37.6380A-6381A.

  1978   "The job interview: Body language and perception of potential effectiveness".
          Journal of Applied Psychology 63:3.388-390.

von Raffler-Engel, Walburga
  1976a   "Linguistic and kinesic correlates in code switching". In William C. McCormack
          and Stephen A. Wurm (eds.), Language and man: Anthropological issues. (World
          Anthropology) The Hague: Mouton, 229-238. (Paper presented at the XIIth
          International Congress of Anthropological and Ethnological Sciences, Chicago,
          Illinois, 1973.)

  1976b   "Some rules of socio-kinesics". In Gerhard Nickel (ed.), Proceedings of the IVth
          International Congress of Applied Linguistics, vol. 2. Stuttgart: Hochschul
          Verlag, 113-121.

  1978   "The structure of nonverbal behavior". Man Environment Systems 8.60-68.

  1980a   "Introduction". In W. von Raffler-Engel (ed.), 1-5.

  1980b   The perception of nonverbal behavior in function of the age and the sex of the
          rater. Arlington, VA: ERIC ED 194 923 CS 503 125. (Paper presented at the
          XXIInd International Congress of Psychology, University of Leipzig, DDR,
          1980.)

  1980c   "Research in the evaluation of nonverbal behavior in the job interview". The
          Linguistic Reporter 22:7.2-3 and 23:11.14.

  1980d   "The unconscious element in intercultural communication". In Robert St.
          Clair and Howard Giles (eds.), The social and psychological contexts of language.
          New York: Lawrence Erlbaum Associates (Wiley and Sons), 101-129.

  1980e   Ethnic body politics in business settings. New York: Institute for Nonverbal
          Communication Research. Audiotape, 90 minutes. (Paper presented at the
          IInd Annual Research Conference of the Institute for Nonverbal Communica-
          tion Research, Columbia University.)

  1981   "Nonverbal factors in minority interviewing". The Kinesis Report 3:3/14.15-18.

  1982   The coordination of verbal and nonverbal interaction towards three parties:
          The analysis of a talk show. Arlington, VA: ERIC ED 220 901 (Paper presented
          in the Main Session, Sub-section 4 on Basic Phenomena of Verbal and Nonverbal
          Interaction, Tenth World Congress of Sociology, Sociolinguistics Section,
          Mexico City, August 16-21.)

1983   "Towards a theory of contact kinesics". In Peter H. Nelde (ed.), Current trends
        in contact linguistics. Bonn, Germany: Ferd. Dümmler Verlag, 239-253. (Paper
        presented at the Second International Symposium on Language Contact and
        Conflict, Brussels, Belgium, Research Center on Multilingualism, 1982.)

von Raffler-Engel, Walburga (ed.)
1980   Aspects in nonverbal communication. Lisse, Holland: Swets and Zeitlinger.
        (Paperback edition in 1983.)

von Raffler-Engel, Walburga and Steven Weinstein
1977   Metakinesic behavior in the description of nonverbal behavior. Trier, Germany:
        Linguistic Agency, University of Trier, Series B, Paper 32.

von Raffler-Engel, Walburga, Amy L. Smith, Roger Cunningham, and Janis Buckner
1978   The use and gestures in consecutive interpretation. Arlington, VA: ERIC ED
        161 173 FL 009 771. (Paper presented at the Fifth International Congress of
        Applied Linguistics, University of Montreal, Canada, 1978.)

von Raffler-Engel, Walburga, Bruce Bennett, Diana Donnelly, Thomas Faulconer, Howard
Freiman, Joseph Herzog, Barbara Johnson, Gregory Puckett, Lucy Richardson, Leonard
Silverstein, Martha Stewart, and Betsy van Vleck
1979   Verbal and nonverbal student interaction in the college classroom as a function
        of group cohesion. Trier, Germany: Linguistic Agency, University of Trier,
        Series B, Paper 2. (Paper presented at the Ninth World Congress of Sociology,
        University of Uppsala, Sweden, 1978.) Idem Arlington, VA: ERIC FL 009
        764 ED 159 916.

von Raffler-Engel, Walburga and Frank Gantz III
1981   "The evaluation of nonverbal behavior in the business interview depending on
        the profession and on the sex of the rater". In Ernest W.B. Hess-Lüttich (ed.),
        Multimedial communication, vol. 1: Semiotic problems and its notation – An
        interdisciplinary approach. (= Kodikas Suppl., 8.) The Hague and Tübingen,
        Germany: Gunter Narr Verlag, 199-214.

von Raffler-Engel, Walburga, Keith Newman, Robin Foster, and Frank Gantz III
1980   "The relationship of nonverbal behavior to verbal behavior in the evaluation of
        job applicants". In W. von Raffler-Engel (ed.), 357-374.

von Raffler-Engel, Walburga, and Steven McKnight
1981   "The perception of nonverbal behavior in function of visible access to one or
        both interactants". In Margot Lenhart and Michael Hertzfeld (eds.), Proceedings
        of the Fifth Annual Meeting of the Semiotic Society of America, Texas Tech-
        nological University, 1980. New York: Plenum Press, 533-542.

Webster, Edward C.
1964   Decision making in the employment interview. Montreal, Canada: McGill Uni-
        versity Relations Centre.

Weisberg, Michael F. and Walburga von Raffler-Engel
1980   The function of repetition in the sales transaction. Arlington, VA: ERIC ED

203 405. (Paper presented at the International Conference on Social Psychology and Language, University of Bristol, England, 1979, and at the Michigan Academy of Sciences, 1980.)

Weitz, Shirley
    1976   "Sex differences in nonverbal communication". Sex Roles 2.175-184.

    1979   "Facial expression and visual interaction". In Shirley Weitz (ed.), Nonverbal communication. New York: Oxford University Press, 18-36.

Wexley, Kenneth N. and Gary A. Yuki
    1977   Organizational behavior and personnel psychology. Homewood, IL: Richard D. Irwin, Inc.

In the PRAGMATICS & BEYOND series the following monographs have been published thus far:

I:1. *Anca: M. Nemoianu*: The Boat's Gonna Leave: A Study of Children Learning a Second Language from Conversations with Other Children.
Amsterdam, 1980, vi, 116 pp. Paperbound.

I:2. *Michael D. Fortescue*: A Discourse Production Model for 'Twenty Questions'.
Amsterdam, 1980, x, 137 pp. Paperbound.

I:3. *Melvin Joseph Adler*: A Pragmatic Logic for Commands.
Amsterdam, 1980, viii, 131 pp. Paperbound.

I:4. *Jef Verschueren*: On Speech Act Verbs.
Amsterdam, 1980, viii, 83 pp. Paperbound.

I:5. *Geoffrey N. Leech*: Explorations in Semantics and Pragmatics.
Amsterdam, 1980, viii, 133 pp. Paperbound.

I:6. *Herman Parret*: Contexts of Understanding.
Amsterdam, 1980, viii, 109 pp. Paperbound.

I:7. *Benoît de Cornulier*: Meaning Detachment.
Amsterdam, 1980, vi, 124 pp. Paperbound.

I:8. *Peter Eglin*: Talk and Taxonomy: A methodological comparison of ethnosemantics and ethnomethodology with reference to terms for Canadian doctors.
Amsterdam, 1980, x, 125 pp. Paperbound.

II:1. *John Dinsmore*: The Inheritance of Presupposition.
Amsterdam, 1980, vi, 116 pp. Paperbound.

II:2. *Charles Travis*: The True and the False: The Domain of the Pragmatic.
Amsterdam, 1980, vi, 116 pp. Paperbound.

II:3. *Johan Van der Auwera*: What do we talk about when we talk? Speculative grammar and the semantics and pragmatics of focus.
Amsterdam, 1980, vi, 116 pp. Paperbound.

II:4. *Joseph F. Kess & Ronald A. Hoppe*: Ambiguity in Psycholinguistics.
Amsterdam, 1980, vi, 116 pp. Paperbound.

II:5. *Karl Sornig*: Lexical Innovation: A study of slang, colloquialisms and casual speech.
Amsterdam, 1980, vi, 116 pp. Paperbound.

II:6. *Knud Lambrecht*: Topic, Antitpoic and Verb Agreement in Non-Standard French.
Amsterdam, 1980, vi, 116 pp. Paperbound.

II:7. *Jan-Ola Östman*: 'You Know': A discourse-functional study.
Amsterdam, 1980, vi, 116 pp. Paperbound.

II:8. *Claude Zilberberg*: Essai sur les modalités tensives.
Amsterdam, 1980, vi, 116 pp. Paperbound.

III:1. *Ivan Fonagy*: Situation et signification.
Amsterdam, 1980, vi, 116 pp. Paperbound.

III:2/3. *Jürgen Weissenborn and Wolfgang Klein (eds.)*: Here and There. Cross-linguistic Studies in Deixis and Demonstration.
Amsterdam, 1982. vi, 296 pp. Paperbound.

III:4. *Waltraud Brennenstuhl*: Control and Ability. Towards a Biocybernetics of Language.
Amsterdam, 1982. vi, 123 pp. Paperbound.

III:5. *Wolfgang Wildgen*: Catastrophe Theoretic Semantics. An Elaboration and Application of René Thom's Theory.
Amsterdam, 1982. iv, 124 pp. Paperbound.

III:6. *René Dirven, Louis Goossens, Yvan Putseys and Emma Vorlat*: The Scene of Linguistic Action and its Perspectivization by SPEAK, TALK, SAY and TELL.
Amsterdam, 1982. vi, 186 pp. Paperbound.

III:7. *Thomas Ballmer*: Biological Foundations of Linguistic Communication. Towards a Biocybernetics of Language.
Amsterdam, 1982. x, 161 pp. Paperbound.

III:8. *Douglas N. Walton*: Topical Relevance in Argumentation.
Amsterdam, 1982. viii, 81 pp. Paperbound.

IV:1. *Marcelo Dascal*: Pragmatics and the Philosophy of Mind. Vol. I.
Amsterdam, 1983. xii, 198 pp. + Index. Paperbound.

IV:2. *Richard Zuber*: Non-declarative Sentences.
Amsterdam, 1983. ix, 123 pp. Paperbound.

IV:3. *Michel Meyer*: Meaning and Reading. A Philosophical Essay on Language and Literature.
Amsterdam, 1983. ix, 176 pp. Paperbound.

IV:4. *Walburga von Raffler-Engel*: The Perception of Nonverbal behavior in the career interview.
Amsterdam, 1983. viii, 148 pp. Paperbound.

IV:5. *Jan Prucha*: Pragmalinguistics: East European Approaches.
Amsterdam, 1983. 120 pp. Paperbound.

IV:6. *Alex Huebler*: Understatements and Hedges in English.
Amsterdam, 1983. 120 pp. Paperbound.

IV:7. *Herman Parret*: Semiotics and Pragmatics. An Evaluative Comparison of Conceptual Frameworks.
Amsterdam, 1983. xii, 136 pp. Paperbound.

IV:8. *Jürgen Streeck*: Social Order in Child Communication. A Study in Microethnography.
Amsterdam, 1983. 120 pp. Paperbound.